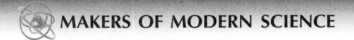

Alfred Wegener

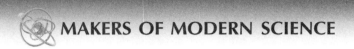
MAKERS OF MODERN SCIENCE

Alfred Wegener

Creator of the Continental Drift Theory

LISA YOUNT

CHELSEA HOUSE
PUBLISHERS
An imprint of Infobase Publishing

ALFRED WEGENER: Creator of the Continental Drift Theory

Chelsea House
An imprint of Infobase Publishing
132 West 31st Street
New York NY 10001

Library of Congress Cataloging-in-Publication Data

Yount, Lisa.
    Alfred Wegener : creator of the continental drift theory / Lisa Yount.
        p. cm.—(Makers of modern science)
    Includes bibliographical references and index.
    ISBN-13: 978-0-8160-6174-7
    ISBN-10: 0-8160-6174-2
    1. Wegener, Alfred, 1880–1930. 2. Geologists—German—Biography. 3. Earth scientists—Germany—Biography. 4. Continental drift. 5. Physical geography. I. Title. II. Series.
    QE22.W26Y68 2009
    550.92—dc22   2008025489

Chelsea House books are available at special discounts when purchased in bulk quantities for businesses, associations, institutions, or sales promotions. Please call our Special Sales Department in New York at (212) 967-8800 or (800) 322-8755.

You can find Chelsea House on the World Wide Web at
http://www.chelseahouse.com

Text design by Kerry Casey
Cover design by Salvatore Luongo
Illustrations by Sholto Ainslie
Photo research by Suzanne M. Tibor

Printed in the United States of America

Bang KT 10 9 8 7 6 5 4 3 2 1

This book is printed on acid-free paper.

to Kat,
who knows far too much about
earthquakes and tectonic shifts

CONTENTS

PREFACE

S cience is, above all, a great human adventure. It is the process of exploring what Albert Einstein called the "magnificent structure" of nature using observation, experience, and logic. Science comprises the best methods known to humankind for finding reliable answers about the unknown. With these tools, scientists probe the great mysteries of the universe—from black holes and star nurseries to deep-sea hydrothermal vents (and extremophile organisms that survive high temperatures to live in them); from faraway galaxies to subatomic particles such as quarks and antiquarks; from signs of life on other worlds to microorganisms such as bacteria and viruses here on Earth; from how a vaccine works to protect a child from disease to the DNA, genes, and enzymes that control traits and processes from the color of a boy's hair to how he metabolizes sugar.

Some people think that science is rigid and static, a dusty, musty set of facts and statistics to memorize for a test and then forget. Some think of science as antihuman—devoid of poetry, art, and a sense of mystery. However, science is based on a sense of wonder and is all about exploring the mysteries of life and our planet and the vastness of the universe. Science offers methods for testing and reasoning that help keep us honest with ourselves. As physicist Richard Feynman once said, science is above all a way to keep from fooling yourself—or letting nature (or others) fool you. Nothing could be more growth-oriented or more human. Science evolves continually. New bits of knowledge and fresh discoveries endlessly shed light and open perspectives. As a result, science is constantly undergoing revolutions—ever refocusing what scientists have explored before into fresh, new understanding. Scientists like to say science is self-correcting. That is, science is fallible, and scientists can be wrong. It is easy to fool yourself, and it is easy to be fooled by others, but because new facts are constantly flowing in, scientists are continually refining their work to account for as many facts as possible. So science can make mistakes, but it also can correct itself.

Sometimes, as medical scientist Jonas Salk liked to point out, good science thrives when scientists ask the right question about what they observe. "What people think of as the moment of discovery is really the discovery of the question," he once remarked.

There is no one, step-by-step "scientific method" that all scientists use. However, science requires the use of methods that are systematic, logical, and *empirical* (based on objective observation and experience). The goal of science is to explore and understand how nature works—what causes the patterns, the shapes, the colors, the textures, the consistency, the mass, and all the other characteristics of the natural universe that we see.

What is it like to be a scientist? Many people think of stereotypes of the scientist trapped in cold logic or the cartoonlike "mad" scientists. In general, these portrayals are more imagination than truth. Scientists use their brains. They are exceptionally good at logic and critical thinking. This is where the generalizations stop. Although science follows strict rules, it is often guided by the many styles and personalities of the scientists themselves, who have distinct individuality, personality, and style. What better way to explore what science is all about than through the experiences of great scientists?

Each volume of the Makers of Modern Science series presents the life and work of a prominent scientist whose outstanding contributions have garnered the respect and recognition of the world. These men and women were all great scientists, but they differed in many ways. Their approaches to the use of science were different: Niels Bohr was an atomic theorist whose strengths lay in patterns, ideas, and conceptualization, while Wernher von Braun was a hands-on scientist/engineer who led the team that built the giant rocket used by Apollo astronauts to reach the Moon. Some's genius was sparked by solitary contemplation—geneticist Barbara McClintock worked alone in fields of maize and sometimes spoke to no one all day long. Others worked as members of large, coordinated teams. Oceanographer Robert Ballard organized oceangoing ship crews on submersible expeditions to the ocean floor; biologist Jonas Salk established the Salk Institute to help scientists in different fields collaborate more freely and study the human body through the interrelationships of their differing knowledge and approaches. Their personal styles also differed: biologist Rita Levi-Montalcini enjoyed wearing chic dresses and makeup; McClintock was sunburned and wore baggy denim jeans and an oversized shirt; nuclear physicist Richard Feynman was a practical joker and an energetic bongo drummer.

The scientists chosen represent a spectrum of disciplines and a diversity of approaches to science as well as lifestyles. Each biography explores the scientist's younger years along with education and growth as a scientist; the experiences, research, and contributions of the maturing scientist; and the course of the path to recognition. Each volume also explores the nature of science and its unique usefulness for studying the universe and contains sidebars covering related facts or profiles of interest, introductory coverage of the scientist's field, line illustrations and photographs, a time line, a glossary of related scientific terms, and a list of further resources including books, Web sites, periodicals, and associations.

The volumes in the Makers of Modern Science series offer a factual look at the lives and exciting contributions of the profiled scientists in the hope that readers will see science as a uniquely human quest to understand the universe and that some readers may be inspired to follow in the footsteps of these great scientists.

ACKNOWLEDGMENTS

I would like to thank Frank K. Darmstadt for his help and suggestions, Suzie Tibor for her hard work in rounding up the photographs, my cats for keeping me company (helpfully or otherwise), and, as always, my husband, Harry Henderson, for—well—everything.

INTRODUCTION

Everything changes. As time passes, Earth and everything on it change. Living things are born and die; species develop, flourish for a while, then evolve into new species or become extinct. The atmosphere, the sea, and even the solid rock of the planet's crust change as well. The floor of a shallow sea is pushed up to become a mountaintop. Mountains are worn down by wind and water and, in time, may sink beneath the waves.

Science changes as well. Scientists observe details of the world around them and make guesses about why things are the way they are and how they might alter in the future. The researchers test these ideas by making further observations or conducting experiments. The results of the tests may confirm the original thoughts or lead to new ones.

In science, as in any other area of human activity, opinions about people and ideas also change over time. Some scientists are hailed as geniuses at first, only to be forgotten later. Others' theories are rejected by their peers but may be brought back to life when new evidence to support them is discovered. Sometimes these positive or negative changes happen within a scientist's lifetime, but, in other cases, researchers' reputations are altered long after their deaths.

A Story of Change

The story of Alfred Wegener and his theory of continental drift is, above all, a tale of change. Wegener's idea, first proposed early in the 20th century, provided a revolutionary picture of the way Earth's surface had changed. Wegener believed that continents had moved together and split apart during the eons of the geologic past, sailing like vast icebergs through a sea of semiliquid rock. Their motion had produced new mountains and islands and opened yawning gaps that filled with ocean water.

Wegener's life was full of change as well. The son of a minister, he chose to become a scientist. He was a pioneer in meteorology, the science that studies Earth's atmosphere and weather, yet a map that reminded him of a jigsaw puzzle led him to venture into geology—a field in which he had no training or experience. He spent most of his time in university towns of Germany and Austria, but he left that quiet existence again and again to explore the white waste of Greenland, where in fact he died.

Finally, the story of continental drift is a story of changes in scientific thinking. During Alfred Wegener's lifetime, fellow scientists respected him as a meteorologist and Arctic explorer, but they ignored or made fun of his theory of moving continents because it was so different from the ideas that most geologists accepted. The drift theory was almost forgotten for three decades after Wegener's death in 1930, and Wegener himself was dismissed as a teller of what one scientific critic called "fairy tales." In the 1960s, however, a cascade of new discoveries about the seafloor led several scientists to resurrect Wegener's ideas and modify them into a new theory called plate tectonics.

Unlike continental drift, plate tectonics had such powerful evidence in its favor that almost all Earth scientists accepted it within a few years. It became part of a new view of Earth as a dynamic, ever-changing system—a "living, mobile thing," as John Tuzo Wilson, one of the architects of the new outlook, said in 1968. Historians writing about this radical change in geology hailed Alfred Wegener, the creator of the tectonics theory's ancestor, as the equivalent of Polish astronomer Nicolaus Copernicus (1473–1543), whose revolutionary picture of the solar system was not accepted in his own time but led to major astronomical discoveries in later eras.

Revolution in Earth Science

In *Great Geological Controversies,* science historian Anthony Hallam called the evolution of geological ideas from continental drift to plate tectonics "one of the most fascinating and best documented [stories] in the history of science." This volume in the Makers of Modern Science set tells that story for young people and profiles Alfred Wegener, the armchair dreamer and daring explorer who started it all. Wegener's life is at the heart of the book, but my account reaches beyond the span of that life to show why Wegener's ideas were so harshly received at first, yet proved so fruitful decades after his death.

Geologists' reactions to Wegener's theory grew out of their beliefs about the nature of Earth and the planet's development. These views were the products of the competing theories and puzzling observations that shaped the science of geology during the 18th and 19th centuries. Chapter 1 of the book provides background on those ideas.

Chapter 2 describes Alfred Wegener's early life and career, up to the time he developed and first published his theory of continental drift. It includes his pioneering meteorological research and his first two expeditions to Greenland. Chapter 3 presents Wegener's theory and the evidence he offered to support it in the fourth and most complete edition of his book, *The Origin of Continents and Oceans.* Chapter 4 tells how contemporary scientists reacted to Wegener's ideas and discusses why most of them rejected his proposals so strongly. Chapter 5 recounts Wegener's last expedition to Greenland, ending with his tragic death on the ice in November 1930, just a day or so after his 50th birthday.

Chapters 6 and 7 trace the path of continental drift theory after Wegener's death. The first part of chapter 6 focuses on the small band of supporters who kept the theory alive during the 1930s and 1940s and modified it in important ways. The second part describes the puzzling observations that reawakened interest in the idea in the 1950s. Chapter 7 describes the torrent of new evidence and proposals that shaped the theory of plate tectonics and led to its rapid acceptance.

The book's conclusion evaluates Alfred Wegener's role as a scientific revolutionary. It also shows ways in which the picture of Earth presented by plate tectonics has altered since the theory's development in the 1960s. It emphasizes that this picture is still being modified today, because change in science, like change in Earth itself, is a process that never ends.

1

Changing Views
of the Earth

Part of being human has always been to wonder . . . to ask questions . . . to try to discover the answers. Some people sought their answers in mythology and religion. Others framed their questions in a different way, which came to be known as science.

Just as people wondered about the sky over their heads and about their own bodies, they wondered about the Earth beneath their feet. What was it made of? How far out and how far down did it extend? Had it always been the way it was now, or was it once different?

Some 2,500 years ago, the ancient Greeks suggested scientific answers to a few questions about the Earth. Aristotle (384–322 B.C.E.), for example, concluded that the Earth was round because it cast a circular shadow on the Moon during lunar eclipses. A later Greek philosopher Aristarchus of Samos (c. 310–230 B.C.E.) described how the planet's daily rotation causes day and night. Eratosthenes of Cyrene (275–194 B.C.E.) even used geometry to

1

calculate the Earth's size around 240 B.C.E. Historians have disagreed about exactly what measurements he used, but, according to one version of his story, he reached an estimate of about 24,389 miles (39,250 km) for the planet's circumference, a figure surprisingly close to the modern estimate of 24,901 miles (40,075 km).

The Greeks disagreed about whether the Earth possessed more than one continent, or large landmass. A globe described in 150 B.C.E. pictured four continents, but in 150 C.E., the astronomer and geographer Ptolemy (ca. 85–165 C.E.) produced a better-known world map that showed only a single, very large landmass. Long-distance land and sea voyages slowly expanded Europeans' knowledge of geography in later centuries, ending with the first sighting of Antarctica—the last of the world's eight continents to be discovered—in 1820. Understanding of how that geography came to be the way it was, however, lagged behind.

Earth's Early Days

Perhaps the first complete theory of Earth's origin, history, and structure that did not grow out of mythology or religion came from the French philosopher René Descartes (1596–1650). In *Principia Philosophae,* published in 1644, Descartes proposed that the planet had started existence as a glowing ball like the Sun and then slowly cooled and hardened. As it lost heat, it also shrank in size. Descartes believed that inner and outer shells of rock, with a thick layer of water between them, covered the Earth's fiery center. Continents emerged when the outer crust broke apart and some segments of it sank into the water. Key elements of this theory—the ideas that the Earth had cooled and contracted during geologic time and that large masses of land, once above water, had sunk beneath the sea—still dominated many geologists' thinking in Alfred Wegener's time.

Several other thinkers offered different ideas about the Earth's past in the late 1700s, when geology began to develop as a science. Perhaps the first was Georges Leclerc, comte de Buffon (1707–88), a respected French scientist who included geology among his many interests. Buffon believed that Earth had been born when a huge comet crashed into the Sun and tore off a flaming mass that became our planet. Like Descartes, Buffon pictured the crust of the early Earth as having several layers, but he placed them in a different order. Buffon imagined water as the top layer, the crust itself in the center, and a honeycomb of huge caves lying beneath it. Eventually the crust cracked, Buffon wrote, and part of the water drained into the caves, revealing what became the continents.

Buffon believed that Earth had once been much warmer, just as Descartes had. He cited as evidence the fossil remains of creatures much like elephants (who lived in the Tropics in his day) found in the chilly far north. Northern areas were once warm enough to support elephants, Buffon said, but, as the planet cooled, they and other tropical animals migrated toward the hotter lands around the equator.

T. Rupert Jones, editor of a British publication called *Geological Magazine,* wrote in 1864 that geology began because people needed to explain how seashells came to be buried in rocks found on mountaintops. Of course Jones was oversimplifying, probably on purpose, but such shells certainly were one of the chief puzzles that early geologists faced. Aristotle had noticed them and guessed that parts of what was then dry land had once lain beneath the ocean. Buffon thought the same thing. "It was no sooner suspected that our continent might formerly have been the bottom of the sea, than the fact became incontestible," he wrote in a book titled *Epochs of Nature* in 1778. "The spoils of the ocean are found in every place."

Other thinkers suggested that the reverse was true: Lands formerly above sea level might have sunk. Another ancient Greek philosopher Plato (427–347 B.C.E.) wrote about a large landmass called Atlantis, which he said had once been the home of an advanced civilization but sank beneath the sea during a catastrophe long ago. Plato probably created his version of Atlantis merely to illustrate his political theories, but he drew on ancient traditions that such lost continents actually existed. Descartes's 1644 account contained no descriptions of lost civilizations, but it carried forward the idea of sinking as well as rising landmasses.

Buffon realized that the kinds of changes he was describing would have taken tremendous amounts of time. The idea that the Earth was ancient, however, went against European religious tradition,

The remains of ancient shells found in land rocks, like these from Chesapeake Bay, were one of the mysteries that puzzled early geologists. The shells suggested that parts of Earth's landmasses had once been under water. (Pam Jeffries/Stockphoto)

which held that the Earth and human beings had been created at the same time. (In one famous age estimate, made around 1650, James Ussher, an Irish archbishop, had analyzed biblical texts and ancient calendar systems and concluded that Earth was created on October 23, 4004 B.C.E.) In what may have been the first attempt to determine the age of Earth scientifically, Buffon measured the cooling rate of red-hot spheres and extended his measurements to reach a figure of about 75,000 years. His observations of fossils made him think that the planet might actually be far older—perhaps as old as 3 million years—but he could find no direct evidence to support that idea and therefore discarded it.

Competing Theories

Two competing theories about the formation of Earth's crust became popular in the decades immediately after Buffon's death. One came from Abraham Gottlob Werner (1749–1817), a respected professor of geology in Freiburg, Saxony (now part of Germany). Like Buffon, Werner believed that water had covered the whole Earth in the planet's youth. Werner said that the crust's earliest rocks had formed when chemicals in the water settled out as solid matter. Later rocks, including those that contained shells and other fossils, were formed from bits of material that drifted down onto the seafloor. Powerful currents in this primeval ocean shaped the crust beneath it into mountains and valleys. Because Werner's ideas stressed the importance of water, his theory came to be known as the neptunist theory, after the Roman god of the sea.

Werner taught many of the best geologists of his day, and his students spread his ideas throughout Europe. Geologists found the neptunist theory appealing because it provided a clear, simple explanation for phenomena that they had observed, such as the fact that different types of rocks were often arranged in layers like a cake. Not everyone agreed with Werner's proposals, however. Some critics said, for instance, that the amount of water currently existing on Earth was too small to have contained all the material that now made up the planet's crust. If there had once been more water, where had it gone?

James Hutton (1726–97), a Scottish businessman with a keen interest in chemistry and geology, was one of the chief opponents of the neptunist theory. Hutton believed that heat deep within the Earth, left over from the planet's fiery beginning, had done more to shape the crust than water had. Because of this emphasis on underground heat, Hutton and his followers were called plutonists, from the Roman god of the underworld.

The Earth's crust, Hutton said, gained its present form through repeated cycles of building up and breaking down. Heat from the planet's interior expanded and pushed up parts of the seafloor, forming new land. Some of the land wrinkled into mountains, including volcanoes, which spewed out fresh rock in liquid form. Wind and water wore down the mountains over time, breaking their rocks into sand and gravel that rivers washed into the sea. The sand and gravel settled on the seafloor, and the underlying heat baked them into solid rock. The same heat eventually pushed up some of this rock to make new mountains, and so on.

Hutton presented his ideas to the Royal Society of Edinburgh in 1785, and the society published them in 1788. In 1795 he expanded his presentation into a two-volume work called *Theory of the Earth with Proofs and Illustrations.* Hutton's theory did not become well known, however, until 1802, when one of his followers, John Playfair (1748–1819), a professor of mathematics at Edinburgh University, described it in a book titled *Illustrations of the Huttonian Theory of the Earth.* Playfair's writing was far more readable than Hutton's difficult prose had been, and his book sold widely.

A number of geological discoveries in the early 19th century supported Hutton's ideas and disproved some of Werner's. Several of Werner's best-known followers therefore abandoned the neptunist theory, and interest in it faded out by the mid-1820s. As one converted British neptunist Adam Sedgwick put it, "For a long while I was troubled with water on the brain, but light and heat have completely dissipated [dispersed] it." Later findings cast doubt on parts of the plutonist theory as well, however. Hutton's true value to geology lay not in this idea but in two others that he put forth in the course of describing it.

James Hutton, a Scottish businessman and geologist, proposed around the start of the 19th century that Earth's geography had been shaped mostly by the planet's internal heat. He stressed that all changes in the Earth during the geologic past were caused by forces that could still be seen in operation, such as erosion. (HIP/Art Resource)

One of these notions was that the Earth was almost infinitely old. Going much further than Buffon, Hutton claimed that geologic time showed "no vestige of a beginning—no prospect of an end." Even more important, Hutton insisted that all geological changes were due to actual causes—forces that could still be seen in operation. "No powers [are] to be employed [in explaining past changes in the Earth] that are not natural to the globe, no action to be admitted of except those of which we know the principle, and no extraordinary events to be alleged in order to explain a common appearance," he wrote. He also stated that "the operations of nature are equable and steady." Playfair expanded on these ideas, for instance pointing out that the pattern of interconnecting valleys running through mountains had the same shape as the pattern formed by a river and its branches. This similarity, he wrote, was evidence that, given enough time, rivers could have carved the valleys by wearing away the mountain rocks.

Catastrophes or Steady Change?

Not all geologists agreed with Hutton that the Earth in the distant past had been essentially the same as it was in their own time. In 1812, Swiss-French scientist Georges Cuvier (1769–1832) stated that the planet had been altered by great catastrophes, including tremendous floods and volcanic eruptions more powerful than anything reported in human history. Cuvier agreed with Hutton that changes on Earth had taken place in cycles and had come through the actions of nature rather than supernatural forces, but he thought that the changes had often been rapid and violent. "It is . . . extremely important to notice that these repeated inroads and retreats [of land and sea] were by no means gradual," he wrote. "On the contrary, the majority of the cataclysms that produced them were sudden."

In support of his claims, Cuvier pointed out that the bodies of elephantlike mammoths, with their skin, hair, and flesh completely preserved, had been found in the permafrost of Siberia. The corpses' condition suggested that they had been frozen very quickly, allowing no time for decay. Further proof came from rock formations, seen in many places, in which the layers were warped and twisted, like a cake dropped onto the floor. "The dislocations, shiftings, and overturnings of the older strata [rock layers] leave no doubt that sudden and violent causes produced the formations we observe," Cuvier wrote.

Alexandre Brongniart (1770–1847) and Léonce Élie de Beaumont (1798–1874), two of Cuvier's followers, developed his ideas further in the 1820s. Dating layers of rock in mountains by means of the fossils they contained, the two men showed that some mountains appeared to be much older than others. Mountain building, they said, had

Charles Lyell (1797–1875): Founder of Uniformitarianism

Charles Lyell was born in Kinnordy, Farforshire, Scotland, on November 14, 1797, the oldest son in a large family. His father, also named Charles, was a lawyer, but one of his interests was botany, the study of plants. Young Charles shared his father's love of nature. He had plenty of opportunities to develop his passion at Bartley Lodge, part of the New Forest area of England, where he spent most of his boyhood.

Lyell followed his father's footsteps into the study of law, earning a B.A. from Exeter College (part of Oxford University) in 1819 and an M.A. in 1821. He began practicing in 1825 and worked as a lawyer for two years. In college, however, the lectures of naturalist William Buckland (1784–1856) had interested him in geology, and he pursued this interest with increasing energy from then on. Wherever he traveled to seek legal cases, for instance, he observed and made notes on the rock formations in the area.

By the time Lyell gave up his law practice in 1827, he had already established a reputation as a geologist. He was elected to membership in the Linnean Society and the Geological Society of London in 1819, the year he graduated from college, and presented his first scientific paper to the Geological Society in 1822. In 1826 he was also elected a fellow of the Royal Society, Britain's premier scientific organization.

Once free to be a full-time author and scientist, Lyell began developing what would become his best-known work, the textbook *Principles of Geology.* Its first edition was published as a three-volume work between 1830 and 1833. Lyell spent much of the rest of his life revising and adding new material to this book; he finished the revision of the first volume of its 12th edition just a few days before his death. He also published a shorter handbook for students, *Elements of Geology,* which first appeared in 1838, and a book about the age and early development of the human race, *Geological Evidences of the Antiquity of Man,* first published in 1863.

Lyell taught geology at King's College, London, from 1831 to 1833. He married Mary Horner, the daughter of a German geologist, in 1832, and she thereafter helped him with his work. He studied the geology of various parts of the world, including Scandinavia, Italy, Spain, Canada, and the United States, and wrote scientific papers about the rock formations he saw in those places.

Mid-19th-century geologist Charles Lyell's doctrine of uniformitarianism, growing out of James Hutton's ideas, stated that all past changes on Earth had been caused by forces now in operation. This belief became a basic principle of geology. Some geologists, however, did not share Lyell's conviction that those forces had always operated at the same rate and intensity that they show at present. (Library of Congress)

He also published travel books about his trips to North America in 1845 and 1849.

Lyell's books sold widely and provided a comfortable income for him and his family. He also received numerous awards for his contributions to geology, including the Royal Medal (1834) and Copley Medal of the Royal Society (1858) and the Geological Society of London's Wollaston Medal (1866). The British government made him a knight in 1848 and a baronet in 1864. Lyell died in London on February 22, 1875, and is buried in Westminster Abbey.

Even more than James Hutton, whose ideas he built upon, Charles Lyell is considered a father of modern geology. He made contributions to many geological subjects, including the study of volcanoes, earthquakes, and glaciers. His ideas about geologic time and change influenced Charles Darwin (1809–82), the creator of the theory of evolution by natural selection, who brought the first volume of Lyell's text on his famous voyage on HMS *Beagle* (1831–36). Although Earth scientists no longer share Lyell's conviction that geological changes always took place slowly and steadily, his doctrine of uniformitarianism is still part of the foundation of geological thinking.

occurred at many different times, probably in sudden bursts of activity. Because of their stress on ancient cataclysms, Cuvier and his supporters became known as catastrophists.

In turn, Charles Lyell (1797–1875), a fellow Scotsman, took up the cause of Hutton and Playfair. Lyell believed that slow cycles of rising and falling land had taken place many times in the geologic past, but there had been no overall change in the planet. He described his ideas in a famous textbook *Principles of Geology*, which first appeared in 1830 and was revised and reissued many times between then and 1872.

Like Hutton, Lyell believed that all past changes in the Earth were caused by processes still in operation. Lyell went beyond Hutton, however, in insisting that those processes had always functioned at the same rate and with the same intensity that they showed in the present day. ("We are not to limit nature with the uniformity of an equable progression," Hutton had written.)

Because Lyell shared Hutton's view that the Earth was very old, he felt that there had been plenty of time for small, gradual changes to produce major effects. He saw no need, therefore, to propose ancient catastrophes. "It appears premature to assume that existing agents could not in the lapse of ages, produce such effects as fall . . . under the examination of the geologist," he wrote. Some past changes, such as those caused by volcanic eruptions and earthquakes, might have been sudden, but they did not need to be any more violent than their modern equivalents. Lyell's view of Earth's history, called uniformitarianism, has often been summed up in the slogan, "The present is the key to the past."

Progressivism

Most geologists were more interested in describing individual rock formations than in speculating about the Earth's past, but those who enjoyed considering broad theories discussed Cuvier and Lyell's ideas vigorously during the 1830s. Many—such as scientist-priest William Whewell (1794–1866), who coined the terms *catastrophism* and *uniformitarianism*—thought that both men might be partly right. They agreed with Lyell that the same *kinds* of forces had shaped the

Earth's crust in the past and the present, but they thought, along with the catastrophists, that those forces might have operated at different rates and intensities at different times. For instance, long periods of quiet might have been punctuated by sudden bursts of cataclysmic geological activity. Alternatively, geological processes might have occurred more quickly or intensely in Earth's early days, when the planet was hotter. The view that the speed or intensity of geological activity might have changed over time was called progressivism.

Although late-19th- and even 20th-century geologists proposed catastrophist theories now and then, progressivism and uniformitarianism came to dominate geological thinking in Europe (including Britain) and the United States by the middle of the 19th century. Conflict between these latter ideas continued, taking on new forms in the second half of the century.

One of the most widely held versions of progressivism, popular since the days of Descartes, focused on the idea that the Earth had been cooling and contracting since its formation. Nineteenth-century supporters of this belief said that mountains formed on the shrinking planet in much the same way that wrinkles form on the skin of an apple as it dries out and shrinks with age. Contraction also forced large blocks of land—even some the size of continents—to sink beneath the sea, separating areas that had once been joined. This idea explained why paleontologists (scientists who study ancient life-forms preserved in rocks) often found fossils of the same kinds of plants and animals in areas separated by vast stretches of water.

Austrian geologist Eduard Suess (1831–1914) summed up this view of the planet in a massive four-volume work called *Das Antlitz der Erde (The Face of the Earth)*, published between 1885 and 1909. Suess suggested that in the Paleozoic era, the time of the earliest life-forms that have left fossils (c. 543–248 million years ago), two huge protocontinents dominated the surface of the Earth. The northern one, for which he borrowed Plato's name of Atlantis, lay where the North Atlantic Ocean now is. The southern continent, which Suess called Gondwanaland (after a native people of India, the Gonds), contained parts of what are now South America, India, and Africa. A central sea, the Tethys, separated the two. The continents took on their present form when parts of Gondwanaland sank beneath the sea. As Suess put it, "The collapse of the world is what we are witnessing."

Suess believed that land and sea had changed places many times during the contraction process. His view was popular in Europe, but most geologists in the United States preferred the theory of permanentism, which James D. Dana (1813–95), a respected professor of geology at Yale University, had set forth in 1846. Dana shared Suess's belief that the Earth had cooled and contracted, but he thought that the continents and oceans had stayed in more or less the same relationship to each other as the planet shrank. Dana pointed out that the fossil shells that had been found on land all belonged to shallow-water species. This meant, he said, that sea level might rise or fall around the edge of continents, but deep ocean basins never rose to become continents, nor did the cores of continents sink. Permanentism was summed up in a popular saying, "Once a continent, always a continent; once an ocean, always an ocean." Although Dana's theory was progressivist in some ways, it was more closely related to Charles Lyell's uniformitarianism. The Earth might have shrunk, Dana said, but in most ways it had changed very little over time.

Floating in a Hidden Sea

Like Descartes and Buffon before them, some 19th-century geologists speculated about what might lie beneath the Earth's crust and how the crust might interact with the layers beneath it. Their theories took a new turn at midcentury because of a strange event that occurred in India around 1840. George Everest, the British surveyor for whom the world's tallest mountain was eventually named, was leading an expedition to measure various aspects of the subcontinent's geology, including the pull of gravity in different places. When he tried his measurements in the Himalayas, he received a considerable surprise.

The more massive an object is, the more strongly it attracts other objects through gravity. A weight swinging freely on the end of a string hangs straight down because gravity pulls it toward the huge mass of the Earth. If other large objects, such as mountains, are nearby, however, their mass will also pull on the weight, moving it sideways by a tiny amount that can be measured. When Everest used this test to measure the gravitational pull of the Himalayas, he found much less sideways movement than he had expected. The gigantic mountains acted as if they were hollow!

The startled Everest sent his results to John Henry Pratt (1809–71), the Archdeacon of Calcutta, who was also a well-known geologist. Pratt calculated that the deflections, or sideways movements, that Everest had observed were indeed less than a third as great as they should have been, given the mountains' mass. Pratt presented his calculations to the Royal Society in 1854.

Pratt's Royal Society paper offered no explanation for his strange findings. A month after he delivered it, however, George Biddell Airy (1801–92), Britain's Astronomer Royal (the country's chief astronomer), sent in another paper that made up that lack. Airy proposed that the Earth's crust was not strong enough to hold up such massive mountains, so the lowest part of them sank down into the layer beneath the crust. The mountains aboveground showed less gravitational pull than expected because part of their mass lay beneath the Earth's surface.

In order for the "roots" of the mountains to sink down in this way, the layer below the Earth's crust had to be soft and yielding, perhaps even something like a thick liquid, Airy said. (The rock walls of deep mines were known to be soft, he pointed out.) If this was the case, then objects floating in the layer should follow the rules that the ancient Greek scientist Archimedes (c. 287–212 B.C.E.) had established for solid objects floating in liquid. The height to which such objects rose above a liquid's surface, Archimedes had said, depended on their mass. Airy compared the different parts of the Earth's crust to logs of different sizes lashed together to form a raft. If one log rose higher above the water than the others, an observer could assume that the bottom of the log would extend deeper into the water by the same amount.

Pratt strongly disagreed with Airy's ideas. In 1861 he put forth an alternative explanation: the differences in gravity and in height came, he said, not from differences in total mass but from differences in density, or mass per unit area. These differences had been built into

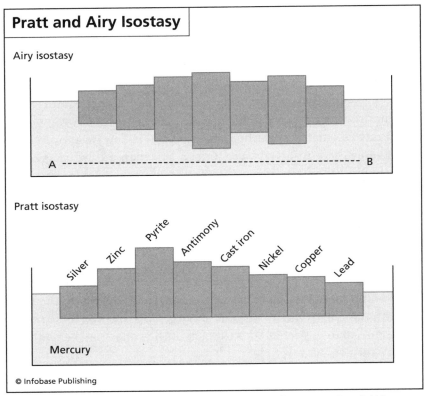

Pratt and Airy Isostasy

Airy isostasy

Pratt isostasy

Mercury

© Infobase Publishing

Two competing theories explained how landmasses might float on a soft or fluid layer beneath Earth's solid crust. Both agreed that objects of different masses would have different heights above the liquid layer. George Airy, Britain's Astronomer Royal, thought that heavier masses would reach both greater heights and greater depths (upper diagram). John Henry Pratt, Archbishop of Calcutta, on the other hand, thought that all the masses would float at an equal depth. Their differences in height occurred because they were made of materials with different densities, or masses per unit volume (lower diagram).

the crust by different rates of expansion and contraction during the planet's cooling. In Pratt's theory, all of the crust's bottom had the same depth, but parts of it rose higher because they were less dense than other parts.

In 1889, Clarence Dutton (1841–1912), a U.S. geologist, coined the term *isostasy* for the balance that both Pratt and Airy described. The word comes from Greek roots meaning "equal standing." Dutton saw isostasy as potentially becoming "geology's unifying theory." The principle of isostasy states that objects floating in a liquid will always achieve a balance between the force of gravity, which pushes them down, and the force of buoyancy, which pushes them up.

Dutton and others went on to show that isostasy provided an excellent explanation for events in which pieces of crust moved up or down—perhaps a better explanation than the rival contraction theory offered. For instance, isostasy predicted that when sediment was deposited on a piece of land, the land should become heavier and sink, perhaps being pushed below sea level. On the other hand, if weight was removed from a landmass, for instance by the melting of an ice cap, the mass would rise. T. F. Jamieson, a British geologist, said in 1865 that Finland and Scandinavia were rising because a gigantic ice sheet that had previously covered northern Europe had melted 10,000 years ago.

After John Hayford and William Bowie, two respected American geologists, showed between 1909 and 1912 that predictions based on isostasy closely matched a series of actual gravity measurements that had been made across the United States, most geologists came to accept that isostasy was real. They were about equally divided, however, about whether Pratt or Airy's theory about it was the correct one.

Most late 19th-century and early 20th-century geologists and geophysicists (members of a new scientific specialty, first developed in the 1870s, that studied the physics and chemistry of the Earth), especially in the United States, also came to accept the related idea that a layer of denser but probably yielding material lay beneath the Earth's lightweight crust. They could not agree, however, on whether the layer below the crust was solid, liquid, or some state in between, like soft tar. Some thought it might be like the ice of a glacier, which is hard and solid to the touch, yet over geologic eons can flow down the side of a mountain like a very slow-moving river.

Eduard Suess believed in the contraction-and-cooling theory rather than isostasy and thought that the layer beneath the crust was solid, but he did accept that such a layer existed. Naming the layers after what he thought were the chief elements that composed them, he called the core *nife* (for the chemical abbreviations for nickel and iron, Ni-Fe), the crust *sal* (silicon-aluminum), and the layer between them *sima* (silicon-magnesium). Suess believed that the sal had migrated upward as the Earth cooled because it was less dense than the other layers. It had originally covered the entire Earth, but parts of it had collapsed and sunk into the sima as the cooling planet contracted, leaving behind the ocean basins of today.

Physical evidence that the Earth had multiple layers appeared in the early 20th century when scientists began measuring the shock waves given off by earthquakes. These waves travel at different speeds in different kinds of material. In 1909, Croatian seismologist (a scientist who studies the way the Earth transmits vibrations from earthquakes and other sources) Andrija Mohorovičić (1857–1936) found a sudden increase in the velocity of primary earthquake waves at a depth of tens of kilometers. This zone, later called the Mohorovicic discontinuity or Moho, came to be considered the boundary between the lower crust and the inner layer now termed the mantle. The Moho lies about 5 miles (8 km) below the ocean floors and an average of 20 miles (32 km) beneath the continents.

The Age of the Earth

A final controversy that shaped geology in the years just before Alfred Wegener proposed his continental drift theory concerned the age of Earth. By the middle of the 19th century, most geologists accepted Hutton and Lyell's belief that the planet was almost infinitely old. They realized that most of the forces that they could see affecting Earth's crust, such as the erosion caused by water and wind, would require hundreds or even thousands of years to show measurable effects. The existence of a very long span of geological time therefore became an essential part of their theories.

Hutton and Lyell had not attempted to give an actual figure for the planet's age or to date past geologic eras, but Lyell's friend and follower Charles Darwin did. In his famous book *On the Origin of Species*, published in 1859, Darwin hazarded a guess that the Tertiary period, the earlier part of the most recent geological era, had begun more than 300 million years ago.

Just three years after Darwin's estimate and partly in reply to it, renowned Scottish physicist William Thomson (1824–1907), better known as Lord Kelvin, announced that the crust of the Earth was only 100 million years old—at most. Kelvin based his opinion on calculations involving the composition and heat conductivity of major rock types in the crust and the increase in temperature with depth that had been measured in mines and similar structures. His views carried a great deal of weight because he was the most famous physicist of his time, the formulator of the laws of thermodynamics, which explain how heat relates to other forms of energy. Physics, in turn, was usually considered to be the most exact of the sciences.

Kelvin reduced his proposed time span even further in later estimates until, in 1897, he stated that the planet was probably only about 24 million years old. Many geologists found this idea distressing because it did not seem to allow enough time for the changes they saw to take place. If the Earth was really that young, they thought, catastrophist theories would have to be revived.

In making his calculations, Kelvin assumed that all Earth's internal heat was left over from its formation and was radiating steadily away. Just as he was issuing his most miserly time estimate, however, scientists in France were discovering a new source of heat: radioactive decay. This phenomenon was first uncovered in 1896, when Henri Becquerel (1852–1908) found that compounds containing the element uranium had a strange ability to darken photographic film. Husband-and-wife physicists Pierre (1859–1906) and Marie (1867–1934) Curie discovered a second radioactive element, radium, and showed in 1903 that it produced heat as well as radiation when it broke down, or decayed, into other elements. A year later, Canadian physicists Ernest Rutherford (1871–1937) and Frederick Soddy (1877–1956) demonstrated that all radioactive elements were unstable, breaking down into other elements and giving off energy in the process. They proposed in 1904 that all radioactive elements, and perhaps all elements, contained huge amounts of energy that could be released when their atoms decayed.

Other scientists went on to discover radioactivity in common rocks, water, and other materials all around the world. It became clear that enough radioactive material existed in the Earth's crust to provide a significant new heat source for the planet. If radioactivity really did heat the Earth, the planet might not be slowly cooling after all. Kelvin's age estimate therefore could be wrong.

Since radioactive decay takes place at steady, measurable rates (different for different kinds of radioactive substances), Rutherford and other scientists proposed that it could be used to determine the age of the Earth more accurately than before. In the early years of the 20th century, after using this method to date individual rock samples, several scientists did just that. They reported that the oldest rocks were up to 2.2 billion years old.

Earth Science in Turmoil

The discovery of radioactive decay also threw into doubt the theory that the Earth was growing smaller over time. If the planet was not losing heat, it might not be shrinking either.

Other questions had been raised about the cooling-and-contraction theory. Some scientists had pointed out, for instance, that contraction ought to produce mountains that were distributed evenly through the crust. Mountains appeared only in certain places, however—usually at the edges of continents. In the late 19th century, furthermore, British scientist Osmond Fisher (1817–1914), a founder of geophysics, had set out to prove Kelvin's assumptions about the cooling and contracting Earth and had found just the opposite. Contraction was simply not powerful enough to raise mountains to the heights that they reached, Fisher said. It ought to produce differences in elevation of no greater than 800 or 900 feet (243.8 to 274.3 m).

In the early 20th century, when Alfred Wegener first proposed his continental drift theory, Earth science was in a state something like that of the planet itself. Parts of it seemed solid, immovable, and ageless, particularly the belief in some degree of uniformitarianism. Just as Earth's crust was divided into many types of rocks and rock formations, Earth science was divided into many specialties that seldom communicated with one another. Mountains of painstakingly gathered knowledge were surrounded by seas of competing theories and unanswered questions: Was Earth cooling and shrinking, or had it maintained its heat and size? Had land and sea changed places in the past, or had they always remained more or less where they now were? What lay beneath the planet's crust, and how did that material behave?

The discovery of radioactivity had recently hit the Earth sciences like a gigantic earthquake or volcanic eruption, shattering many long-held assumptions. Geologists, geophysicists, and scientists in related specialties were still struggling to grasp what this new information implied. Most felt far from ready to deal with another such explosion.

Weather Pioneer

2

Neither science nor adventure played any part in Alfred Lothar Wegener's background. Wilhelm Wegener, his great-grand-uncle, was a friend of the great German explorer Alexander von Humboldt, but Wilhelm Wegener himself had been a minister. Alfred Wegener's father, Richard, was a minister as well. He also ran the Schindler Orphanage from 1875 to 1904. This orphanage was not the dismal home for poor children portrayed in Charles Dickens's novels, but rather a private institution and school for the sons of civil servants, clergymen, and teachers. Perhaps Wegener's mother, Anna, identified with their plight, since she herself had lost her parents at an early age.

An Active Youth

When science and adventure moved into the Wegener family, it arrived in a double dose. Both Alfred, born in Berlin on November

1, 1880, and his brother, Kurt, two years older, grew up to become meteorologists in the pioneering days of that field, when learning about the Earth's atmosphere often involved excitement and risk. Alfred and Kurt were two of Richard and Anna Wegener's three surviving children; the third was their sister, Tony. Two other siblings had died in childhood. Of all these children, Alfred was the youngest.

Little is known of Alfred and Kurt's childhood, except that they often spent time at their family's vacation home in Zechlinerhütte, a small country village in northern Germany, about 50 miles (80.5 km) north of Berlin. (Their mother had been born, as Anna Schwarz, in that same village.) The boys' love of the outdoors probably developed during these country stays. Perhaps less enjoyably, they went to high school at the Cöllnischen Gymnasium in Berlin, from which Alfred graduated in 1899.

Alfred and Kurt were certainly leading active, athletic lives by the time they entered college. They went hiking and climbing in the Alps during a summer together in Innsbruck, Austria, in 1901, for instance. A few years later, while visiting a friend in the mountains, Alfred learned to ski as well.

As has happened to many college students before and since, the Wegener boys' activity occasionally spilled over into trouble. According to Martin Schwarzbach's *Alfred Wegener: Father of Continental Drift*, the only full-length biography of Wegener in English, Alfred was arrested and fined for "gross misconduct and disturbing the peace" during his freshman summer at the University of Heidelberg in 1900. A police officer named Eiermann arrested him because, the officer reported, "at 3 a.m. [Wegener] paraded down the main street to the market square wrapped in a white sheet and shouting loudly in an unseemly manner."

In spite of a few such wild nights, Wegener did well during his college years. He did the bulk of his studying at the University of Berlin, then called Friedrich Wilhelm University. He also spent one summer each at the Ruprecht Karl University in Heidelberg and the University of Innsbruck. He studied mathematics and natural sciences, with a focus on meteorology and astronomy. After earning a bachelor's degree in 1901, he took time off for a required year of military service. He then began graduate studies in astronomy, meanwhile working at the Urania Society's observatory in Berlin.

For his doctoral thesis, Wegener translated reference charts called the Alfonsine Tables from their original form, which used the number 60 as a base, to the decimal (base 10) form used by everyone in his own day. These tables had first been developed in 1273 under the patronage of a Spanish king, Alfonso X of Castile, for use in calculating the positions of the Sun, the Moon, and the five planets known in those times. Ship captains made such calculations as part of their navigation duties.

Meteorology: The Science of Weather

Humans have always tried to predict the weather because their lives depended on it. Weather made crops flourish or fail; weather determined which ships would reach port safely and which would sink in a storm. For most of history, though, people could do little more than watch the sky and pass on what they observed in proverbs such as "Red sky at morning, sailors take warning."

Perhaps the first person to try to turn weather prediction into a science was Aristotle. Around 340 B.C.E. he wrote a book called *Meteorologica,* which means "the study of things that fall from the sky or are suspended in the air." This included not only what are now called meteors, but also clouds, rain, and snow. Since Aristotle lacked equipment to measure such things as air pressure and temperature, it is probably not surprising that most of his ideas about weather were wrong.

Tools for measuring phenomena in the atmosphere began appearing in the 17th and 18th centuries. Italian mathematician and physicist Evangelista Torricelli (1608–47) invented the mercury barometer, which measures air pressure, in 1643. Low pressure, he observed, usually meant that a storm was on the way. British scientist Robert Hooke (1635–1703) created an anemometer, a device for measuring wind speed, in 1667. Gabriel Fahrenheit (1686–1736), a German physicist, invented the mercury thermometer and created a temperature scale to go with it in 1714. (A second scale, the centigrade or Celsius scale, was devised by Swedish astronomer Anders Celsius (1701–44) in 1742. A year later, a French scientist modified the scale into its present form, which sets the

Wegener received his Ph.D. from the University of Berlin on November 24, 1904, magna cum laude, for this work. He went on to write an article on the history of the venerable tables as well. Nonetheless, he must have found his thesis project boring, because he concluded soon afterward that his future did not lie in astronomy. He later summed up his objections to that science in these words:

> *In astronomy everything has essentially been done. Only an unusual talent for mathematics together with specialized*

---

freezing point of water as 0° and the boiling point of water as 100°.) Swiss geologist and meteorologist Horace de Saussure (1740–99) invented the hair hygrometer for measuring humidity in 1780.

Even with all these devices, large-scale weather prediction was not practical until weather data and warnings about dangerous events such as storms could be transmitted quickly over long distances. Samuel F. B. Morse's (1791–1872) telegraph made such communication possible beginning in 1844. Shortly afterward, several countries set up networks of weather stations, connected by telegraph, that sent their information to central bureaus. These bureaus, in turn, combined the stations' data to make weather maps and forecasts. In the United States, for instance, the Smithsonian Institution established a national weather observation network of 150 stations in 1849. Britain founded the first national meteorological service in 1854, and daily weather forecasts began appearing in British newspapers in 1860.

By the dawn of the 20th century, when Alfred and Kurt Wegener were choosing their careers, the study of weather (short-term changes in the atmosphere) and climate (changes that cover larger areas and longer periods of time) was just beginning to be considered a true science. The fact that the atmosphere had more than one layer had been discovered only in 1902, for instance. A Norwegian scientist Vilhelm Bjerknes (1862–1951) pointed out in 1904 that weather prediction could be made through mathematical calculations based on the laws of physics. After that time, meteorology became more closely integrated with other physical sciences.

installations at observatories can lead to new discoveries; and besides, astronomy offers no opportunity for physical activity.

Arctic Explorer

Leaving astronomy behind, Wegener turned to his other chief scientific interest, meteorology, which seemed to offer much more exciting possibilities. Kurt (who had studied meteorology at a different university) was already working as a technical aide at the Royal Prussian Aeronautical Observatory in Lindenberg, a suburb of Berlin, and Alfred joined him there in 1905.

Like other investigators at the observatory, the Wegeners used kites and balloons to learn about the atmosphere. These floating devices had been essential tools for weather investigators for several centuries. Meteorologists had realized that they could understand weather and climate only by measuring such things as temperature and wind speed at different heights in the atmosphere, and kites were one of the first tools they used to carry measuring instruments into the air. Perhaps the most famous weather kite was the one that American statesman and inventor Benjamin Franklin (1706–90) flew in 1752, with a key attached, to try to find out whether lightning was a form of electricity. Other scientists tied thermometers to kites and sent them up to measure temperatures at various altitudes.

When Joseph (1740–1810) and Jacques (1745–99) Montgolfier, two French brothers, invented the hot air balloon in 1783, the infant science of weather gained another useful aid. Balloons tethered to a cable could carry instruments high into the air and be easily retrieved. People could also ride in balloons filled with hot air or hydrogen gas to make more elaborate measurements or experiments. At the time the Wegener brothers joined the Aeronautical Observatory, kites and balloons were the chief tools that meteorologists used to investigate the upper atmosphere.

Not content with the observatory's unmanned balloons, Alfred and Kurt Wegener learned ballooning. On April 5–7, 1906, they represented the observatory in the Gordon Bennett Contest for Free Balloons. They won the contest by making a 52-hour unbroken flight from Bitterfeld, in central Germany, to Jutland, in northern Denmark,

Balloons were (and sometimes still are) used to carry instruments into the atmosphere to obtain data on weather and climate. Alfred Wegener used weather balloons like this in his work at the Royal Prussian Aeronautical Observatory and on his expeditions to Greenland. (Archive/Alfred Wegener Institute)

and then back to a more southerly part of central Germany near Frankfurt. Their journey set a new record for the longest continuous time that a balloon carrying human beings had remained in the air, beating the previous world record by 17 hours.

Floating in the peaceful skies above Germany was not enough to satisfy Alfred Wegener's lust for adventure. Since childhood he had wanted to follow the trail of such famous explorers as Fridtjof Nansen (1861–1930) into the ice-filled wilderness of the Arctic, and later in 1906 his experience with balloons brought him his first chance to do so. He was hired as the meteorologist for the *Danmark* expedition, a 28-man exploration of northeast Greenland. Ludvig Mylius-Erichsen (1872–1907), a Danish scientist, was the expedition's leader.

Most of Greenland, the world's largest island, is anything but green (although in the Middle Ages, when Scandinavian settlers first came there, it may have been warmer and, therefore, greener than it is today). Washed by chilly currents from the Arctic and Atlantic Oceans, it has an Arctic climate. More than four-fifths of it is covered by an ice sheet. This massive ice cap, which is said to represent 10 percent of the world's freshwater reserves, is 2.5 miles (4 km) thick in places. Its weight has pushed down the central part of the island into a basin that lies more than 1,000 feet (300 m) below sea level.

The *Danmark* expedition was largely concerned with learning about the life of the icy island's Native people, the Inuit. Wegener nonetheless had the chance to send kites and captive balloons as high as 9,843 feet (3,000 m) to make observations about Greenland's weather. In doing so, he became the first person to use weather kites and balloons to collect high-altitude data in a polar climate. He and other expedition members also made an extensive and dangerous journey across the island's largely unmapped northeast coast, sometimes traveling by dogsled and sometimes using sledges that they dragged themselves.

Wegener's student and fellow Greenland explorer Johannes Georgi wrote in Schwarzbach's *Alfred Wegener* that the *Danmark* expedition allowed Wegener "to put into practice all his physical and intellectual abilities, his scientific knowledge, and his practical skill for the exploration of the upper layers of the atmosphere in the Arctic, for meteorological investigations of all kinds, for astronomy, meteorological optics, and glaciology." It also showed him firsthand how unforgiving the Arctic environment could be. Mylius-Erichsen and two other team members died during the expedition's first winter, when they made a foray away from the group's base camp and ran out of food before they could find their way back. In spite of this loss, the rest of the expedition team, including Wegener, stayed on and completed the planned exploration's second year, returning in 1908.

Grim as parts of the expedition were, Wegener felt completely fulfilled in this icy, beautiful land. "Out here, there is work worthy of a man; here, life takes on meaning," he wrote in his journal. He spoke even more poetically of the Arctic in an article he authored on his return:

> Alexander von Humboldt states somewhere in his writings that there is so little of interest in the polar regions

that expeditions there are not worthwhile. If he could have stood as we did, under the flickering northern lights, with an overwhelming feeling of insignificance at the sight of this phenomenon of nature, . . . he would never have said such a thing. Above us the shining curtain unfolded in mysterious movements, a powerful symphony of light played in deepest, most solemn silence over our heads, as if mocking our efforts: Come up and investigate me! Tell me what I am!

Popular Teacher and Writer

Shortly after his return to Germany, Wegener began work on a textbook, *Thermodynamik der Atmosphäre (Thermodynamics of the Atmosphere).* The book described how heat interacts with

Alfred and Else Wegener are seen here in their home in Marburg, soon after their marriage in 1913. Else was the daughter of Wegener's mentor, climatology expert Wladimir Köppen. (Neuruppin Museum, August-Bebel Strasse 14-15, Neuruppin, Germany)

In 1909, Alfred Wegener became a Privatdozent at the University of Marburg, shown here. The university did not give him a salary; students who wanted him to teach them paid him directly. (Thomas Becker/Stockphoto)

other variables, such as air pressure and moisture, in the Earth's atmosphere. Late in 1908 he sent a copy of his manuscript to Wladimir Köppen, an eminent meteorologist then working at the German naval observatory in Hamburg, for review. According to Johannes Georgi, Köppen at the time was considered the "grand old man of meteorology."

Wegener had asked Köppen's advice once before, just before his 1906 Greenland expedition, when Köppen had been head of the meteorological kite station at Grossborstel, near Hamburg. Their contact at that time had been brief, but after they consulted on Wegener's thermodynamics textbook, Köppen became the younger man's close friend and mentor. He also introduced Wegener to his daughter, Else, who was just 16 years old in 1908, when the two first met. Else was greatly struck by this handsome young man 12 years older than herself: "He was still tanned from the Arctic Sun and the sea air," she recalled later in a book she wrote about Wegener. "His gray-blue eyes beamed light from his dark face." Apparently the attraction was mutual: The two would marry five years later.

Meanwhile, the papers that Wegener wrote about his kite and balloon observations in Greenland led the University of Marburg to hire him in 1909 to teach meteorology and astronomy. He was not a full faculty member, but rather what was called a *Privatdozent.* This meant that the university did not pay him a salary; instead, he had to try to earn a living from fees given him by students and people who hired him to give lectures. According to university records cited by Martin Schwarzbach, Wegener taught classes in such subjects as the physics of the atmosphere, atmospheric optics, and "astronomic-geographic position-finding for explorers."

Wegener's students seem to have liked him. Johannes Georgi, who began studying under him in 1910 and went on to become a fellow Arctic explorer and close friend, described his teacher as "a man of medium height, slim and wiry, with a face more often serious than smiling, whose most notable features were the forehead and the stern mouth under a powerful, straight nose." Georgi went on to say that Wegener "quickly won [his students'] hearts by the firm yet at the same time modest and reserved manner in which he immediately introduced them to the fundamentals" of meteorology. Wegener explained complex subjects in a clear and simple manner that students found easy to understand, Georgi recalled,

A photograph of Alfred Wegener was taken in 1910, when he was about 30 years old. At that time he was teaching at Marburg and writing a textbook about the way heat interacts with other variables, such as air pressure and moisture, in the Earth's atmosphere. (Foto Marburg Art Resource)

yet he never talked down to them. He often enlivened his lectures with tales of his Greenland adventures.

Wegener's thermodynamics textbook was published in 1911, and several well-known meteorologists praised it. Wladimir Köppen wrote that the book showed Wegener's "special talent for explicating difficult problems simply and clearly with a minimum of mathematics, and yet with no loss of precision." Although Martin Schwarzbach points out that, at 30 years old, Wegener was young to be writing such a work, the text became very popular and went through several editions. Indeed, according to Roger McCoy's *Ending in Ice,* a biography of Wegener that focuses on his Greenland expeditions, Wegener's book became "the standard textbook for atmospheric physics in Germany" in the 1910s and 1920s.

Wladimir Köppen (1846–1940): Pioneer Climatologist

Wladimir Peter Köppen was born in St. Petersburg, Russia, on September 25, 1846. His grandfather, a physician, had moved there from Germany in 1786 to work for the Russian government under the rule of Catherine II (Catherine the Great, 1729–96). His father was a well-known geographer, historian, and expert on ancient Russian cultures.

Like Alfred Wegener, his future son-in-law, Wladimir Köppen was unusual for his time in being an expert in several scientific fields. He studied botany, zoology, physics, and climatology at the Universities of St. Petersburg, Heidelberg, and Leipzig. He obtained his Ph.D. in botany from the University of Heidelberg in 1870.

After working for several years in the Russian meteorological service, Köppen moved to Germany in 1875 and became chief of the new marine meteorology division of the German naval observatory in Hamburg. His first job was to set up a weather forecasting service for northwestern Germany and the nearby seas. He left the marine meteorology office after four years, but he continued to work for the naval observatory as a researcher until 1919, when he retired and Wegener replaced him.

Köppen applied all his scientific interests to his greatest achievement, a system for classifying the world's climates that is still used

A Bizarre Idea

During this same period, Wegener had the inspirations that would lead to his most long-lasting achievement: the theory of continental drift. He wrote later that his first thoughts on the subject came around Christmas 1910 when he looked at a world atlas that a friend had received, perhaps as a holiday gift. He was struck by the fact that the outlines of Africa and South America looked as though they could fit together like the pieces of a jigsaw puzzle. "Doesn't the east coast of South America fit exactly against the west coast of Africa, as if they had once been joined?" he wrote in a letter to Else. "The fit is even better if you look at a map of the floor of the Atlantic and compare the edges of the drop-off into the ocean basin

in a modified form. He recognized that climate determined what types of plants would grow in an area and that vegetation, in turn, could be used as a marker for climate. Relating vegetation patterns to measurements of rainfall and air temperature, he divided the world into five climate zones: tropical humid, dry, temperate/mild midlatitude, continental/severe midlatitude, and polar. (University of Wisconsin geographer Glen Trewartha later added a sixth zone, the highland.) Köppen first published his climate classification scheme in 1884 but continued revising it for most of his life. The first complete version appeared in 1918, and the final version was published in 1936, when he was 90 years old.

Köppen also investigated Earth's climates during past geological eras, a field called paleoclimatology. This subject interested Alfred Wegener as well, and the two wrote a famous book about it, *Die Klimate der Geologischen Vorzeit (The Climates of the Geological Past)*, which was published in 1924. In addition, Köppen wrote several volumes of a massive *Handbuch der Klimatologie (Handbook of Climatology)*, which he coauthored with his student Rudolf Geiger, and several hundred scientific papers. This venerable and productive scientist certainly lived up to his personal motto, "without haste and without rest." He died in Graz, Austria, on June 22, 1940.

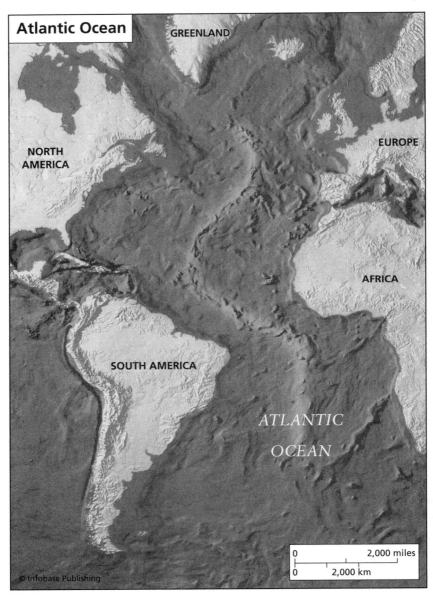

While looking at an atlas that a friend had received as a Christmas present, Alfred Wegener noticed that the shapes of South America and Africa looked as though the two continents could once have fitted together like puzzle pieces, although they are now separated by the Atlantic Ocean. This observation was the inspiration for Wegener's theory of continental drift.

rather than the current edges of the continents. This is an idea I'll have to pursue."

Wegener was not the first person to notice this apparent match. Roger Bacon (1561–1626), a British statesman and philosopher, had remarked on it almost 300 years before. Alexander von Humboldt, the friend of Wegener's great-granduncle, had mentioned it in his writings as well. Antonio Snider-Pellegrini, an American living in France, also had published a book in Paris in 1858 called *La création et ses mystéres dévoilés (Creation and Its Mysteries Unveiled)*, which included a diagram in which a proto-American continent that he called *Atlantide* (Atlantis) was snuggled up against the west side of Africa; Australia was equally cosily tucked under the bulge of Africa's eastern side. This arrangement, Snider-Pellegrini said, explained why fossil plants from the Carboniferous period (354–290 million years ago) in Africa and the Americas were so much alike. None of these men, however, had discussed this in any detail or explained in scientific terms what it might mean. At the time his idea struck him, Wegener wrote later, he had never heard of these earlier writings.

In spite of his words to Else, Wegener soon dismissed his thought about the continents having been joined as being, as he wrote later, "improbable." Most geologists, he knew, believed that the continents had always remained in the same positions on the planet, though parts of them might have been pushed upward or sunk beneath the sea from time to time in the geologic past. His strange thought surfaced again in the fall of 1911, however, when—quite by accident, he wrote—he happened to see a book describing fossil animals that had lived in West Africa and Brazil during the Paleozoic era, 542 to 251 million years ago. He read with amazement that some of the fossils from both places were nearly identical. The book's author, like many other geologists of the time, explained this and other similarities by saying that the continents had once been connected by land bridges that later sank below sea level. What Wegener knew of geophysics made him doubt this idea. Suddenly the alternative—the notion that the continents had moved horizontally over time—no longer seemed so wild.

The Wegener family shown on a balloon ride, a rare family outing, on April 17, 1912. Left to right are Alfred; Kurt, his older brother; Else Köppen, his fiancee; and Tony, his sister. (Foto Marburg Art Resource)

During the next few months, Wegener gathered information from a variety of scientific fields to support his theory. Almost from the beginning, he was sure his ideas were right, even though they contradicted what most Earth scientists of the time believed. He wrote to Köppen on December 31, 1911, "If it turns out that sense and meaning are now becoming evident in the whole history of the Earth's development, why should we hesitate to toss the old views overboard? Why should this idea be held back for ten or even thirty years?"

Wegener first presented his proposal in two speeches given at different scientific meetings in January 1912. He made the first talk, "The Geophysical Basis of the Evolution of the Large-Scale Features of the Earth's Crust (Continents and Oceans)," on January 6 to the Geological Association in Frankfurt. Four days later, he gave the second, "Horizontal Displacements of the Continents," to the Society for the Advancement of Natural Science in Marburg. He combined the speeches into two papers that were published later in the year.

Love and War

Wegener's theory attracted little attention at this time, and exciting turns in his own life soon forced him to set it aside. The first of these events was a long-awaited chance to return to Greenland. In 1912 he joined a four-man expedition led by Johan Peter Koch, a Danish explorer who had been with him on the *Danmark* trip. The expedition began with a two-and-a-half-week stay on Iceland, an Arctic island much smaller than Greenland, during which they crossed the island (including its mostly unexplored largest glacier, the Vatnajökull) twice "for practice." They used Icelandic ponies, which Koch was planning to take to Greenland for transportation instead of dogs. Koch hoped that the ponies would be able to climb the steep slopes of Greenland's huge glacier more easily than Mylius-Erichsen's dogsleds had succeeded in doing.

After arriving in Greenland in the late summer of 1912, Koch's party spent the winter on the eastern edge of the inland ice cap; they were the first explorers to winter on the ice sheet itself. Then, beginning in April 1913, they made a two-month journey across the sheet at its widest part, a distance of 746 miles (1,200 km). Using 16 Icelandic ponies, they scaled the steep inland glacier, climbing as high as 9,843 feet (3,000 m) and narrowly avoiding the huge chunks of ice that repeatedly broke free of the main mass. The group finally reached the island's west coast, but they lost all their ponies and almost starved before an Inuit group rescued them on July 15. This was the longest crossing of the ice cap on foot that had been undertaken up to that time.

Alfred Wegener returned to Greenland in 1912 and 1913 as part of a small expedition led by Danish explorer Johan Peter Koch. Wegener is shown here at the expedition's camp in Borg, Greenland. (Bildarchiv Preussicher Kulturbesitz/Art Resource)

Much of Wegener's work on this expedition, he said later, consisted of taking photographs of weather-related phenomena, such as clouds, ice, and the spectacular northern lights. He also gathered weather and climate data throughout the winter. On his return, he helped Koch prepare a book on the expedition and on Greenland's climatology and glaciology, *Durch die Weisse Wüste* (*Across the White Wilderness*), which was published in 1919. "The account of this journey is and will remain a classic of the exploration of Greenland," wrote Johannes Georgi, who had accompanied Wegener and Koch on the trip. In 1913, Wegener received a Danish medal, the Knight's Cross of the Order of Danebrog, for his part in the expedition, and the *Gesellschaft für Erdkunde* (Geological Association) in Berlin also awarded him and Koch their Carl Ritter Medal.

Shortly after his return from Greenland, Wegener married Else Köppen, who by then was 21 years old. Their first child, Hilde, was born in 1914. The long shadow of war soon fell over these happy events, however: World War I began on July 29, 1914, and Wegener, a reserve lieutenant in the Queen Elisabeth Grenadier Guards' Third Regiment, was called to active duty in Belgium immediately. Kurt, for his part, became a fighter pilot.

According to a colleague, Professor Benndorf, Wegener had mixed feelings about his service: he was loyal to his country, but he felt that war was pointless. Nonetheless, he saw enough action to be wounded twice later in 1914, first in the arm and later, two weeks after he had returned to the battlefront, in the neck. Although he continued to serve in the military meteorological service, he was relieved of active duty for the remainder of the war. During the time he spent at home recovering from his wounds, he turned once more to the theory he had been forced to set aside and began gathering the additional evidence he would need to flesh it out into a book.

Continental Drift

3

Alfred Wegener published *Die Entstehung der Kontinente und Ozeane (The Origin of Continents and Oceans),* the first complete version of his continental drift theory, in 1915. He revised the book extensively three times, adding to the evidence supporting his theory each time; the revised editions appeared in 1920, 1922, and 1929. The 1922 edition was translated into several languages, including an English edition, which appeared in 1924. The version most available in English today is a 1966 retranslation of the fourth (1929) edition, the final version issued during Wegener's lifetime. Fifth and sixth editions, edited by Kurt Wegener, were published after Alfred's death.

The basic concept in Wegener's theory was the one that had gripped him from the beginning—the idea that the Earth's continents had moved horizontally on the planet's surface during past geologic eras. In doing so, they had changed their shape, their position on the surface, and their relationship to each other and the ocean basins. Wegener's term for this motion, the German word *verschiebung,* would be most accurately translated as *displacement.* The theory nevertheless became known in English as *continental drift.*

A Challenge to Geology

Wegener's theory was controversial from its beginning because it contradicted two other theories that many Earth scientists of his time accepted. One was the idea that some present-day continents had formerly been connected by land bridges that later sank beneath the sea. Paleontologists liked this theory because it explained why identical or closely related species of living or fossil plants and animals often appeared in widely separated parts of the world. These creatures seemed unlikely to have crossed the oceans that currently separated them or to have evolved so similarly in separate places.

The sinking of such large areas was thought to be possible because of a second widely held geological belief: the idea that in its youth, the Earth was both hotter and larger. As the planet cooled, supporters of this theory believed, it shrank, causing its crust to wrinkle. The wrinkling pushed some areas up, forming mountain chains, and forced others below water level.

Wegener did not accept either of these theories, and he pointed out recent scientists' objections to both. The discovery of radioactivity offered a new possible heat source for the Earth, he said, so the planet's core need not be cooling. The shrinkage theory could not explain why mountains had formed at different times or why mountain chains appeared only in certain places.

In turn, if the Earth was not shrinking, there was no reason for large landmasses to have disappeared beneath the oceans. Wegener claimed that the widely accepted principle of isostasy also ruled out the idea of large sunken landmasses. Such masses would be too buoyant to sink unless a large weight were placed on them, he said, and he knew of no geological activity that would have provided such a weight.

Geologic Time

Drawing on measurements of radioactive decay in rocks from the Earth, the Moon, and elsewhere in the solar system (meteorites), Earth scientists today have concluded that the Earth, like the rest of the solar system, is about 4.5 billion years old. Geologists divide this expanse of time into a timescale with units of several sizes.

The largest divisions in the geological timescale are called eons. Each eon is divided into eras, and each era is split into periods. Smaller divisions within periods (epochs, ages, and chrons) are also used. Traditionally, the geological timescale is shown with the oldest time at the bottom and the most recent time at the top, so that it resembles the way layers of rock are stacked in the Earth's crust.

Alfred Wegener's description of continental drift involves only the later part of the Phanerozoic eon—the time during which multicellular living things with body parts hard enough to have formed fossils have existed on Earth. In the following table, eras and periods are shown only for this eon.

Eon	Era	Period	Time Span (millions of years ago)
Phanerozoic	Cenozoic	Neogene	23–present
		Paleogene	65.5–23.0
	Mesozoic	Cretaceous	146–65.5
		Jurassic	200–146
		Triassic	251–200
	Paleozoic	Permian	299–251
		Carboniferous	359–299
		Devonian	416–359
		Silurian	444–416
		Ordovician	488–444
		Cambrian	542–488
Proterozoic			542–2,500
Archaean			3,800–2,500
Hadean			3,800–4,500

Note: Alternatively, the Cenozoic era is sometimes divided into the Tertiary period, dating from 65.5 to 2.6 million years ago, and the Quaternary period, from 2.6 million years ago to the present. (The terms primary and secondary were once applied to earlier eras, but they are no longer used.)

As an alternative to the theory of sinking land bridges, Wegener noted, some geologists accepted James D. Dana's proposal that land and sea had changed places only around the edges of continents. Wegener did not completely agree with this permanentist theory either. Yet powerful geophysical evidence, such as the evidence for isostasy, supported Dana's idea, just as biological evidence supported the land bridge theory. If either concept were rejected, the facts that favored it would have to be reinterpreted.

Wegener maintained that continental drift provided the new explanation that was needed. The idea that the continents had moved horizontally over geologic time fitted with the facts supporting both of the other theories, he claimed. It also resolved the contradictions between them. In the fourth edition of *The Origin of Continents and Oceans* he wrote:

> *If drift theory is taken as the basis [of understanding the Earth's history], we can satisfy all the legitimate requirements of the land-bridge theory and of permanence theory. . . . There were land connections, but formed by contact between blocks now separated, not by intermediate continents which later sank; there is permanence, but of the area of ocean and area of continent as a whole, . . . not of individual oceans or continents.*

Ancient Continents

Wegener wrote that in the Paleozoic era, more than 250 million years ago, all of the Earth's crust that reached above sea level was gathered into a single huge continent. In the second and third editions of his book, he called this protocontinent *Pangaea*, meaning "all-Earth." It occupied about half of the planet's surface area and was surrounded by a single shallow ocean, *Panthalassa* ("all-sea").

Pangaea broke up and its fragments slowly separated from each other during the Mesozoic era, Wegener claimed. In the Jurassic period, it split into three smaller protocontinents, two northern ones and a southern one. One of the northern continents was more or less the same as present-day Asia; the other consisted of what is now North America, Greenland, and Europe. Wegener did

Continental Drift

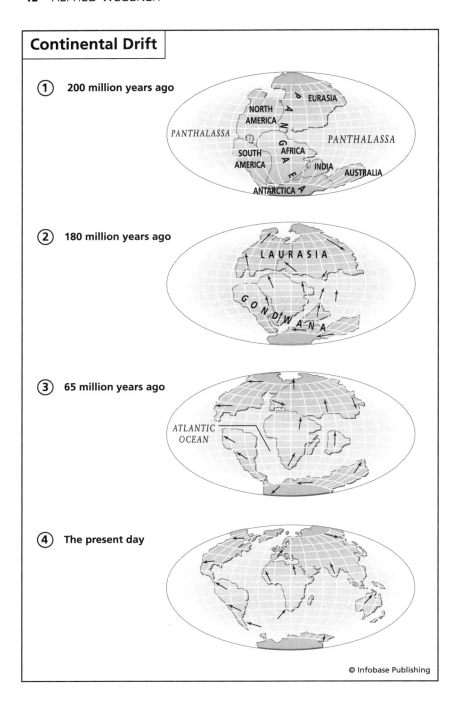

① 200 million years ago

② 180 million years ago

③ 65 million years ago

④ The present day

© Infobase Publishing

Another "Continental Drift" Theory

Frank Bursley Taylor (1860–1938), a geologist who worked for the U.S. Geological Survey, published a theory of continental movement somewhat like Alfred Wegener's in 1910, two years before Wegener presented his first talk on continental drift. Taylor's chief interest, however, was not continents but mountains. His theory was intended to explain the origin of the large, curved mountain ranges on the eastern and southern borders of Asia, which continued into the Mediterranean region. All these mountains, including the Alps and the Himalayas, had arisen at about the same time in the relatively recent geologic past (Mesozoic era).

Taylor rejected the idea that these mountains had been formed because the Earth had cooled and contracted, as Eduard Suess and many other geologists believed. "The Earth never was a molten globe. The whole idea is pure Cartesian [from René Descartes] fiction," he wrote in a later version of his theory, published in 1926. "Its internal temperature has been substantially constant for unnumbered ages." Instead, he said, the mountains resulted from massive movements of Earth's crust that began after the planet's gravity captured a comet in the Cretaceous period (144–65 million years ago). The comet became our Moon. This cataclysmic event flattened the formerly spherical planet at the poles and increased its speed of rotation. The gravitational pull of the new Moon, much closer to Earth than it is now, also created powerful tides.

Taylor proposed that all of the Earth's land had originally existed as two protocontinents centered over the north and south poles. The effects of the Moon's capture made these supercontinents break up. Most of the pieces drifted toward the equator in what Taylor called

(continues on next page)

(Opposite page) *According to Alfred Wegener's continental drift theory, all of Earth's landmasses were once part of a single supercontinent that he called Pangaea (all-Earth). Pangaea began breaking up about 200 million years ago (1). By 180 million years ago, Pangaea had split into a northern and a southern landmass (2). Borrowing a term from an earlier researcher, Wegener called the southern continent Gondwana. A later scientist, Alexander du Toit, named the northern continent Laurasia. The widening Atlantic Ocean separated the Americas from Africa about 65 million years ago (3). India had broken free from Africa but had not yet attached itself to Asia. The continents are still changing positions slowly today (4). For instance, the Atlantic Ocean is widening.*

(continued from previous page)

"a mighty creeping movement," much as ice sheets crept down some of the continents in later times. Some of the masses collided with obstacles, pushing up "wrinkles" that became mountain ranges. The Himalayas and India's Pamir plateau arose, for instance, when part of the southward-moving former northern continent ploughed into the ancient mass of the Indian subcontinent.

In their wake, Taylor's account continued, the moving continents left great tears or rifts in the crust that became the basins of the Arctic, South Atlantic, and Indian Oceans. The Mid-Atlantic Ridge, a chain of gigantic undersea mountains known to run north and south down the center of the Atlantic Ocean, marked the rift created when Africa separated from South America. Taylor also said that Greenland, Canada, and northern Europe had once been joined. The North Atlantic now occupies the space that opened up between them.

Taylor did not work out the movements of the continents in detail, and he presented little geological evidence to support his proposals. His ideas about the Moon, furthermore, were probably too much like catastrophism for geologists' comfort. Because of these failings, his theory, presented to a meeting of the Geological Society of America on December 29, 1908, and published in the society's *Bulletin* in July 1910, attracted little attention.

Alfred Wegener mentioned Taylor in the fourth edition of his book, but he wrote that he had not heard of Taylor's theory at the time he developed his own ideas. Wegener's theory was certainly much more complete and more carefully supported than Taylor's. Although some American geologists called continental drift "the Taylor-Wegener theory" at first, Taylor's version was ultimately forgotten.

not name these continents, but for the southern protocontinent, made up of Africa, South America, India, Australia, and Antarctica, he borrowed Eduard Seuss's name of Gondwanaland (or simply Gondwana). He wrote that Gondwana, in turn, began to break up in the Cretaceous period, but the pieces of the northern block remained together until late in the Cenozoic era, perhaps 3 million years ago. As the blocks of land separated, they tended to move westward and toward the equator.

A Moving Island

Because Wegener's drift theory contradicted several widely held geological beliefs, he knew that he would need a great deal of evidence to convince other scientists that his idea had merit. In the two decades between the first formulation of the drift theory and his death, he assembled supporting facts from a wide variety of Earth sciences, including geodesy (the measurement of the size and shape of the Earth), geophysics, geology, paleontology, and paleoclimatology. This breadth was highly unusual in a time when scientists rarely stepped outside their own specialized fields of study. "All Earth sciences must contribute evidence towards unveiling the state of our planet in earlier times," Wegener wrote in the foreword to the fourth edition of his book.

Wegener used most of his book to describe this evidence. He admitted that all of it was indirect: It fitted with or supported his theory but did not prove it. "We are like a judge confronted by a defendant who declines to answer, and we must determine the truth from the circumstantial evidence," he wrote in the foreword to the book's fourth edition. "All the proofs we can muster have the deceptive character of this type of evidence." In spite of this limitation, Wegener believed that the quantity and variety of his evidence were so great that they amounted to proof.

Wegener organized his facts according to the different Earth sciences from which they came, devoting a chapter to each scientific branch. He began with geodesy, which involves precise measurements of latitude and longitude. The *Danmark* expedition had made such measurements in Greenland in 1907, and earlier scientists had made similar ones at almost the same spots in 1823 and 1870. Greenland's movement away from Europe, Wegener said, was expected to be the fastest among current landmasses. Since the movement was in an east-west direction, it would be shown by increases in the difference in longitude between the two lands.

Wegener admitted that these measurements might not be completely accurate. First, they had not all been made at exactly the same spot, although he said they had been adjusted to correct for this problem. Second, the measurers had determined time of day, an essential part of the calculations, by referring to charts of the Moon's position in the sky. Such charts were less accurate than time signals transmitted by radiotelegraph, which geodesists were beginning to use in the 1920s. Even so, Wegener felt that these early figures were precise enough to be valuable, especially when they were grouped with two more from scientists in 1922 and 1927 who did use radiotelegraphy.

Put together, Wegener said, all these measurements showed that Greenland was gaining longitude (moving westward) relative to Greenwich in Britain, the arbitrary zero longitude point, at the rate of 118 feet (36 m) a year. This increase was nine times as large as the average error expected in the observations. *"The result is therefore proof of a displacement of Greenland that is still in progress,"* Wegener wrote (the italics are his). He offered sets of latitude and longitude measurements for several other continents and islands that also appeared to show movement of the landmasses. Geodesic figures like these were the best evidence that parts of Earth's crust had moved in the past, Wegener claimed, because they demonstrated that such movement was still occurring.

Two Layers of Crust

Turning to geophysics, Wegener presented evidence to support the idea that the Earth's outer shell has two layers. First, he said, measurements of the crust's heights and depths, including what little was known about the parts under the ocean, fell into two main statistical groups: continental tables, averaging 755 feet (230 m) above sea level, and deep seafloors, about 15,420 feet (4,700 m) below sea level. Very few figures fell in between. In other words, continental shelves extended under shallow seas and then dropped off abruptly to the depths of the true ocean floor. "In the whole of geophysics there is probably hardly another law of such clarity and reliability as this—that there are two preferential levels for the world's surface," Wegener wrote.

Wegener also provided several reasons for thinking that the two layers were made of different materials. One reason came from measuring seismic waves, or waves of force given off by earthquakes. These waves travel through different kinds of rock at different speeds. They had been shown to move through the rocks of the ocean floor about 0.062 miles (0.1 km) per second faster than through the rocks of the continents. Geomagnetic research had also shown that the rock of the ocean floor was more easily magnetizable than most continental rock and therefore probably contained more iron. Finally, samples of rock obtained in deep-sea dredging had usually proven to be basalt, a dense, iron-containing rock believed to have come directly from the Earth's molten interior. Basalt was seldom found on land except as part of the lava thrown out of volcanoes.

Using terms slightly modified from those coined by Eduard Suess, Wegener called the two layers of the Earth's crust *sial* and *sima.* He wrote that *sial* (a term he thought was less confusing than *sal* because *sal* is also the Latin word for "salt") is relatively light-weight and composed mainly of rocks related to granite. All the land above sea level, as well as the continental shelves under the shallow seas near coastlines, is sial, Wegener said. The sial layer of the continents is about 62 miles (100 km) thick. On the ocean floors, by contrast, this layer is very thin—about 3 miles (5 km) thick at most—or perhaps even nonexistent. The sima layer beneath the sial consists mainly of basalt, which is denser and heavier than the granitelike rocks that make up sial.

Wegener, like a number of geologists, believed that the sima, even though made of solid rock, acted like a thick, or viscous, liquid. Such an idea might seem strange at first, he admitted, but he gave several examples of solids that behave like thick liquids under some circumstances. The Earth might seem as hard as steel, but even steel can flow like a liquid under great heat and pressure, Wegener pointed out. Pitch, a form of petroleum, also sometimes acts like a solid—shattering under a hammer blow, for instance—but it sags slowly as gravity acts on it over time. "The Earth behaves as a solid, elastic body when acted upon by short-period forces such as seismic waves," Wegener wrote. "However, under forces applied over geological timescales, the Earth must behave as a fluid."

Support for the idea that the sima acted like a viscous liquid also came from the widely accepted geophysical concept of isostasy,

Wegener said. If the lower layer of crust was soft enough to permit the rising and falling movements thought to be caused by isostasy, such as the uplift of Scandinavia, he saw no reason why it should not allow horizontal movements as well. The movements would be almost imperceptibly slow, but over the ages of geologic time they could occur if some force impelled them. Wegener, the Arctic explorer, wrote that pieces of sial (continents and islands) floated on and moved through the sima layer as icebergs move through the polar oceans. The sluggish sima slowly gave way before the moving blocks of sial and then closed up behind them, much as syrup or honey does if a person drags a finger through it.

Matching Rocks

Wegener offered extensive arguments from geology to support his idea that certain continents had once been joined together in larger landmasses. If the edges of the continents had once lain side by side, he wrote, rock formations that had developed before the separation should be similar on both sides of the break, just as the edges of a photograph ripped in half would show similar light and dark areas because they had once been part of a single picture. In fact, Wegener said, this was the case in certain places. The match between rock formations in the Cape Mountains of South Africa and the Sierra de la Ventana, mountains lying just south of Buenos Aires, Argentina, was especially striking, he noted. Vast, rocky plains found in South Africa and Brazil were also very similar. The resemblances between these plains included pipes of kimberlite and related minerals that produced valuable diamonds for both countries.

In much the same way, matching formations on opposite sides of the North Atlantic showed spots where North America and northern Europe had once been attached like conjoined twins, Wegener claimed. For instance, he believed that the Appalachian mountain chain of eastern Canada and the United States was a continuation of a worn-down chain that covered parts of southwest Ireland and Brittany, a part of France. He said that another ancient mountain range, the Caledonian, had matching parts in the Scottish Highlands and northern Ireland on one side and Newfoundland, part of Canada, on the other.

To Wegener, these detailed matches in rock formations provided some of the strongest evidence for drift theory. He wrote the following:

> *The conjunction brings the continuation of each formation on the farther side into perfect contact with the end of the formation on the near side. It is just as if we were to refit the torn pieces of a newspaper by matching their edges and then check whether the lines of print run smoothly across. If they do, there is nothing left but to conclude that the pieces were in fact joined in this way.*

Suppose, Wegener's book said, that the first pair of matching formations—the Cape mountains of South Africa and the sierras of Buenos Aires—made the odds 10 to one that the drift theory was correct. Since at least six independent matches of this type were known, Wegener claimed that the odds went up to 10^6, or 1 million to one, in drift theory's favor. "These figures may be regarded as exaggerated, but they should show the significance of a plurality of independent tests," Wegener wrote.

Still other geological formations showed different stages in the process of continental splitting, Wegener said. The first stage was visible in narrow, deep rift valleys such as those seen running north and south through East Africa. These rifts slowly widen and deepen and, when they reach the edges of the continents, eventually fill with ocean water.

Wegener believed that both mountains and islands resulted from continental movement. Some mountain ranges, such as the Himalayas and the Tian Shan of China, came from crumpling produced as the edges of continental blocks collided. Others, including the ones that line western North and South America and continue around the rim of the Pacific Ocean to form the Ring of Fire, were produced as the leading edges of continental blocks plowed through the resisting sima.

Trailing edges of the continental blocks, on the other hand, often broke off and remained struck in the ocean floor as the continents continued on, forming groups of islands that have an easily recognizable curving (arc) shape. Volcanoes usually appear along the inner side of the curve. The bulging outer side, by contrast, shows earthquake faults and, often, deep ocean trenches. Wegener said that the Malayan archipelago (group of islands), off southeastern Asia, is the most striking example of an island arc.

Separated Twins

Just as certain rock formations on different continents showed a degree of similarity that only drift theory could easily explain, fossil plants and animals in many of the same places showed equally striking resemblances, Wegener went on. He claimed that the continental drift theory could account for these matches at least as well as the popular theory of sunken land bridges. A type of fern called *Glossopteris* and a family of small Permian reptiles named mesosaurs were among the fossil twins he mentioned. *Glossopteris* fossils appeared in India, Australia, South America, South Africa, and

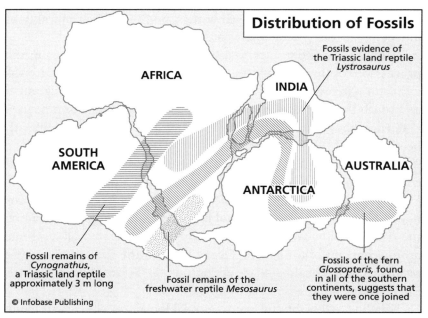

Nearly identical fossils of certain plants and animals can be found on several continents now separated by vast oceans. Alfred Wegener believed that the fossils were so similar because the continents were once part of a single southern continent, Gondwana. Some of the fossils whose distribution impressed Wegener the most are shown here.

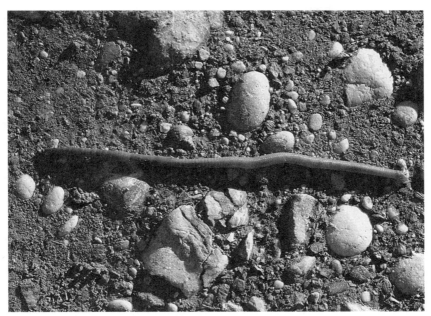

Earthworms obviously cannot swim across oceans, but very similar species of earthworms are found in Europe and the northeastern areas of North America. Wegener believed that this similarity provided further evidence for his continental drift theory. (Goga, 2008, Shutterstock, Inc.)

Antarctica—the same landmasses that Wegener said had once made up the southern supercontinent of Gondwana. Mesosaur fossils were found only in South Africa and Brazil.

Paleontological connections between Europe and northeastern North America were less clear, but Wegener wrote that types of organisms possessing closely related species in both places included earthworms, pearl mussels, perch (a type of fish), garden snails, and heather (a brushy plant). In the case of the snails, which are found widely in western Europe and the British Isles but elsewhere only in Labrador, Newfoundland, and the eastern United States, he commented:

> *The theory of sunken continents ... must interpolate a very long hypothetical bridge in order to connect the two small areas of distribution; with the accumulation of such cases, it becomes increasingly unlikely that the eastern and western boundaries of the distribution would have lain just on today's*

Except for one species of opossum that lives in North America, marsupials (pouched mammals) like this Australian brushtail possum are found only in Australia and South America. Alfred Wegener felt that this distribution of animals indicated that the two continents once were joined. (Sandra Caldwell, 2008, Shutterstock, Inc.)

continents rather than on the wide continental bridge—that is, in today's ocean.

Living organisms show similarly odd distributions, Wegener said. He wrote that compared to the animals of the Sunda Islands, part of the Malay Archipelago lying just north of Australia, the animal life of Australia "is like something so foreign as to have come from another world!" According to him, the animal species thought to have been on Australia the longest, which are found mostly on the southwestern part of the continent, show relationships with the animals of India, Ceylon, Madagascar, and southern Africa. This reflects Australia's connection with those lands, which ended when Gondwana began to break up at the start of the Jurassic period. The marsupials, or pouched mammals, so characteristic of Australia and some South Pacific islands arrived later and appear mainly in only one other area—South America. (One species of opossum lives in North America.) Even the marsupials' parasites are nearly identical in the two places, as Wegener noted. "I believe that the Australian fauna [animals] will provide the most important material that biology can contribute to the overall problem of continental drift."

Fossil Climates and Wandering Poles

By the time Wegener assembled the last edition of his book on continental drift, he and his father-in-law, Wladimir Köppen, had also written their book on paleoclimatology. Some of their discoveries in this field also supported drift theory, Wegener believed. In addition, they fitted with the idea that in previous geological eras, the Earth's internal axis had shifted, causing the planet's North and South Poles to "wander" to locations different from their present ones. This change would have altered the climate of various areas substantially.

Wegener described several kinds of evidence that reveal the fossil climates that different continents had experienced in the past. One is the traces of former inland ice sheets left in the form of rock deposits called tillites. Seams of coal, considered to be fossilized peat beds—packed masses of decayed plant material—offer another. Thick masses of coal mean heavy plant growth under damp (swampy) conditions, which suggests a tropical climate. Minerals that form underwater but are later found on land, reflecting changes in sea level, provide a third climate indicator.

The distribution of fossil plants and animals also offers indirect evidence of changes in climate, Wegener wrote. For example, Spitsbergen, an island north of Scandinavia (part of Norway), now has a polar climate and is buried under inland ice. Fossils from the early Tertiary period taken from Spitsbergen, however, show several kinds of trees that grow in temperate climates, such as pines, beeches, and oaks. Still further back in time, in the Jurassic and early Cretaceous periods, sago palms—a tropical plant—grew in this now-frozen land. Wegener also stated that all the present southern continents, as well as the Deccan area of India, had glaciers at the end of the Carboniferous period and the beginning of

The fact that the southern continents, most of which now have tropical climates, were largely covered by glaciers like this one in the late Carboniferous and early Permian periods suggested to Alfred Wegener that the South Pole had once lain under southern Africa. All those continents, then part of Gondwana, would therefore have had a polar climate. Alfred Wegener climbed this particular glacier, the Vatnajökull in Iceland, at the start of his Greenland trip with Johan Koch in 1912. (Vera Bogaerts, 2008, Shutterstock, Inc.)

the Permian. They therefore must have had a polar climate at that time. By contrast, none of the present northern continents had glaciers then.

Wegener maintained that this glacier evidence also offered strong support for the idea of polar wandering. He believed that at the time the southern glaciers existed, the South Pole lay more or less under the center of the protocontinent Gondwana. The North Pole, on the other hand, was under the Pacific Ocean, so no land was close enough to be affected by its climate. He also pointed out that a huge, thick belt of coal, the remains of plants deposited during the Carboniferous period, stretches across North America, Europe, Asia Minor, and China. This is exactly where the equatorial climate, with its constant rain and year-round heavy plant growth, would have been if the poles were in the location Wegener described. He wrote:

> Not only the Permo-Carboniferous traces of glaciation, but also the total climatic evidence of that period falls into place with the application of drift theory and forms a climatic system which corresponds completely to that of today, provided the South Pole is displaced to southern Africa. With the present-day position of the continents, however, it is altogether impossible to combine the data into an intelligible system of climates. These observations therefore constitute one of the strongest proofs of the validity of drift theory.

"The overwhelming majority of geologists" accepted the idea that there was a considerable displacement of the North and South Poles during the Tertiary period, Wegener claimed. He went on to discuss the concept of polar wandering in more detail. He defined it as a movement of the Earth's whole crust relative to its lower layers, representing an internal shift in the planet's axis.

The Motors That Drive the Continents

Toward the end of his book, Wegener considered possible forces that could produce the movement of landmasses he was proposing. He admitted that he could not explain the causes of continental drift very well. This did not worry him, however, because he felt that the evidence that drifting had in fact occurred was so overwhelming. "The Newton of drift theory has not yet appeared," he wrote, referring to the British scientist Isaac Newton (1643–1727), who had explained the law of gravity. Wegener added, "His absence need cause no anxiety." He was sure that later research would reveal the motor that drove the crust's movement.

The only two mechanisms Wegener could think of were what he called "flight from the Poles" (*Pohlflucht*) and tidal effects in the crust. Hungarian physicist Loránd Eötvös (1848–1919) had first described *Pohlflucht* in 1913. It was caused, Eötvös said, by centrifugal force from the Earth's rotation and by the bulge at the slightly flattened Earth's equator, whose increased gravity pulled landmasses toward it. The tides could produce friction that dragged on the Earth's crust, slowing the crust's rotation and making it move westward relative to the interior. Both *Pohlflucht* and tidal drag are very weak forces, Wegener admitted, but he believed that over the eons of geologic time, their effects could be significant.

A third possible mechanism, for which evidence was just beginning to be accepted at the time Wegener prepared his final edition, was convection currents in the sima. These currents occur in a liquid or gas that contains areas at different temperatures. Imagine a pot of water sitting on the burner of a gas stove, for instance. The burner's flame heats the water immediately over it first, making the molecules in that area move faster. This increased movement causes the water in that spot to expand and rise. When the hot water reaches the surface of the liquid, the colder air above it makes it cool down again. More hot water rising from below pushes the cooler water toward the sides of the pot, where it contracts and sinks downward. The water is thus in constant motion as parts of it continually change places.

Heat from the Earth's interior was expected to make the sima hot. Some geologists believed that this heat radiated easily from the deep seafloors, where only a thin layer of hardened rock separated the sima from the chilly ocean waters. It built up, however, under the thicker blocks of crust that made up the continents. This uneven heating would make sima rise up beneath the continental blocks, flow along them to their edges, then cool and sink as it passed beneath the oceans. Friction caused by these currents might break up the continents, Wegener thought.

Alfred Wegener felt he had assembled an impressive collection of reasons for believing that the continents could move around the Earth's surface. It remained to be seen whether other Earth scientists would accept his revolutionary idea.

"Utter, Damned Rot"

4

Alfred Wegener returned to Marburg in 1918, after World War I ended in Germany's defeat. He and Else had a second daughter, Käthe, that year; a third, Charlotte, arrived two years later.

Wegener's family, like most Germans, had to deal with shortages of food and other necessities for a while. Wegener's academic life, on the other hand, prospered. Wladimir Köppen retired from his post at the German Marine Observatory in 1919 (though he would continue to remain active in science for many decades), and the observatory chose Wegener to replace his father-in-law as director of their department of theoretical meteorology. Wegener, Else, and their daughters therefore moved into the lower floor of the Köppens' house in Hamburg, while Wladimir and his wife, Marie, moved upstairs. Wegener was also reunited with his brother when Kurt became the head of another department at the observatory in that same year.

One of Wegener's accomplishments during his years in Hamburg was a book on the origin of the Moon's craters, published in 1921. He wrote, correctly, that the craters came from the impacts of meteors, not volcanic eruptions as some other geologists thought. He also authored a number of papers on meteorology as well as the second and third editions of his book on continental drift. He gave lectures at the University of Hamburg as well. In 1922, he and another scientist Erich Kuhlbrodt went on a sea voyage to Cuba and Mexico and measured upper air currents over the Atlantic. Knowledge about these air currents was expected to be important once transatlantic air travel became common.

Most important, Wegener and his father-in-law worked together on a book called *Die Klimate Geologischen Vorzeit (Climates of the Geological Past)*, a pioneering work in paleoclimatology that was published in 1924. Its picture of ancient climates was closely tied to Wegener's continental drift theory, which Köppen, after being skeptical at first, had come to accept. According to Martin Schwarzbach, "No one before . . . had offered as thorough and consistent an interpretation of the Earth's climatic history" as the two men did in this book.

In spite of these achievements, Wegener was frustrated. Time after time he applied for a professorship at German universities but was turned down. His friend and former student, Johannes Georgi, believed that these rejections occurred because

This photograph shows Alfred Wegener in 1925, soon after he became a professor at the University of Graz (Austria). Geologists were strongly criticizing his continental drift theory at this time. (Bildarchiv Preussicher Kulturbesitz/Art Resource)

Wegener's work strayed outside of his own field of meteorology, a dangerous behavior in that era of rigid specialization. Wegener's continental drift theory, furthermore, had made him a controversial figure both in his own country and overseas, and most universities did not welcome mavericks.

Austria proved more understanding than Germany. In 1924, the University of Graz offered Wegener a professorship in meteorology and geophysics that it had created just for him. He accepted, and his family and the Köppens moved to Graz. They soon became Austrian citizens. Else Wegener wrote later that the family's years in that university town, within sight of the Alps, were the happiest of their lives. During Wegener's years in Graz, his research focused mostly on continental drift and on plans for further exploration of Greenland.

Early Reactions to Drift

It was fortunate that Wegener found personal fulfillment in these posts, because his drift theory was sailing through rough seas. Neither his 1912 papers nor his 1915 book had been well received in German-speaking Europe. In 1918, for instance, Fritz Kerner-Marilaun (1866–1944), a highly regarded Austrian paleoclimatologist, referred sarcastically to the "delirious ravings of people with bad cases of moving crust disease and wandering pole plague." On the other hand, Émile Argand (1879–1940), founder of the Geological Institute of Neuchâtel, Switzerland, and an expert on the Alps, defended the drift theory at an international geological meeting in 1922 because he felt that it explained certain puzzling features of those mountains. For the most part, although Wegener's book attracted enough interest for him to publish revised and expanded editions in 1920 and 1922, Germanic geologists simply ignored his proposal.

Philip Lake, a British geologist, provided one of the first major reactions to Wegener's theory in the English-speaking world. Lake reviewed the second edition of Wegener's book for *Geological Magazine* in August 1922. This review, and a speech on the same subject that Lake gave to the Royal Geographical Society in London in January 1923, presented many of the same objections that later critics would make. To begin, Lake protested that Wegener "is not seeking truth; he is advocating a cause and is blind to every fact that tells against it." In other words, Wegener was violating the unwritten rule that a scientist's public writing should appear to be objective rather than openly favoring any theory, even the researcher's own.

Lake admitted that Wegener was "a skillful advocate and present[ed] an interesting case." However, Lake doubted that continents could move horizontally, particularly under the forces Wegener had proposed. He questioned data such as the height statistics that Wegener gave to show that the Earth's crust had two layers. He also pointed out that in order to achieve the neat fit that appeared in his maps, Wegener had altered the present-day outlines of the continents a great deal. Lake wrote:

> It is easy to fit the pieces of a puzzle together if you distort their shapes, but when you have done so, your success is no proof that you have placed them in their original positions. It is not even a proof that the pieces belong to the same puzzle, or that all of the pieces are present.

Lake found Wegener's matches between widely separated mountain ranges such as the Caledonian folds of Scotland and the mountains of eastern Canada equally unconvincing. The supposedly matching rocks of South Africa and South America, he said, had not yet been mapped well enough to show whether they were really similar or not. Lake pointed out that *Glossopteris* fossils and signs of glaciers in the Permian and Carboniferous periods appeared, not only in the places Wegener had mentioned, but also in spots such as northeastern Persia, northern Russia, Siberia, and North America, which did not fit with Wegener's maps at all.

Most of the Royal Geographical Society scientists who discussed Wegener's ideas after Lake's presentation basically agreed with Lake. Several thought that horizontal movement of the continents might be possible, but they doubted that Wegener's description of it was correct. Even so, they felt that Wegener should receive credit for having proposed a thought-provoking idea. At the end of the discussion, the president of the society, the Earl of Ronaldshay, concluded

> The impression left on my mind by the discussion is that geologists, as a whole, regret profoundly that Professor Wegener's

hypothesis cannot be proved to be correct. . . . Some theory of this kind is required to explain facts which have long been known to geologists and while they feel bound to condemn this particular hypothesis . . . they still hope that some other hypothesis of a kindred nature will be discovered which will satisfy their requirements.

Rejection in America

Unlike the earlier versions of Wegener's book, the third (1922) edition was translated into other languages. When the English edition appeared in 1924, most Earth scientists outside the German-speaking world learned about Wegener's theory for the first time. Some, such as Harold Jeffreys (1891–1989), an eminent geophysicist at Britain's Cambridge University, did not like what they saw any better than Lake had. Jeffreys stated, for instance, that *Pohlflucht* and tidal forces were a million times too weak to move the continents.

British scientists' reaction to Wegener's ideas was mild, however, compared to opinions in the United States. American Earth scientists expressed their feelings especially vigorously at a meeting sponsored by the American Association of Petroleum Geologists that was held in New York City on November 15, 1926. This conference, the first international meeting to discuss Wegener's theory, was titled "Theory of Continental Drift: A Symposium on the Origin and Movement of Land-masses both Intercontinental and Intracontinental, as Proposed by Alfred Wegener." Twelve scientists—nine Americans (including Frank Taylor, author of a rival drift hypothesis) and three Europeans—attended. Perhaps fortunately for him, Alfred Wegener was not among them. However, he did send in a short paper offering clarification and new data on two topics discussed in his book.

A few of the scientists at the meeting favored Wegener's theory, or at least its basic idea—that the continents had moved horizontally on the Earth's surface during the geological past. One supporter was the meeting's chairman, an influential Dutch oil geologist named W. A. J. M. van Waterschoot van der Gracht (1873–1943). Van der Gracht's long introduction and conclusion speeches, both defending continental drift, took up more than half the pages of the book containing the printed version of the meeting's papers. He pointed out difficulties with the currently accepted theory that the Earth had cooled and contracted and urged geologists to be open to other possibilities. Chester Longwell of Yale University, one of the attendees, said that he was not hostile to the idea of continental movement but doubted much of Wegener's evidence. He commented

> [The theory's] daring and spectacular character appeals to the imagination both of the layman and of the scientist. But an idea that concerns so closely the most fundamental principles of our science must have a sounder basis than imaginative appeal.

Most of the meeting's speakers, by contrast, strongly opposed the continental drift theory. They reserved their harshest criticisms for Wegener's suggestions about the forces that had made the continents move. They agreed that pole-fleeing force and tidal drag both existed. They doubted that these tiny forces could have shifted massive pieces of rock, however, no matter how much time they had had in which to do so.

Harsh Criticisms

The scientists at the New York meeting did not question the existence of the sial and sima layers in the Earth's crust, but they pointed out that researchers still had not agreed on the extent, nature, and qualities of either layer. It was especially unclear whether the sima acted more like a liquid or like a solid. Furthermore, retired Stanford University geologist Bailey Willis (1857–1949) complained, Wegener was trying to have it both ways: If the sima was weak, or liquid, enough to allow the continents to plow through it, how could it at the same time be strong enough to crumple the continents' leading edges into mountains? William Bowie of the U.S. Coast and Geodetic Survey (1872–1940), another eminent Earth scientist who attended the meeting, similarly asked why, if the sima was such a weak layer, the ocean floor could maintain the ridges and trenches that it was known to possess, rather than being completely flat.

Other conference members brought up other questions. Paleontologist Charles Schuchert (1856–1942) of Yale University wondered why Pangaea had survived geological periods marked by great unrest in the Earth's crust, only to break up in a time that was supposed to have been geologically quiet. J. W. Gregory (1864–1932), an Australian geologist working in Britain, pointed out that some similarities between animals and plants in western North America and Asia were just as striking as those between Africa and South America, yet a connection between those continents was not part of Wegener's scheme.

As Philip Lake and some of Wegener's German critics had done earlier, speakers at the 1926 meeting fired criticisms at every class of evidence that Wegener had found so convincing. The geodetic measurements of Greenland's longitude—even the ones using radiotelegraph time signals—were too inaccurate to show whether the island was moving, they said. They made the same criticisms of Wegener's distorted outlines of the continents that Lake had done. Regarding the supposed matches between rock formations and fossils on different continents, they accused Wegener of having picked out data that fitted his theory while ignoring other equally well-documented facts that did not.

Powerful Feelings

All these criticisms were important, several historians of science who have written about the continental drift controversy say, but they should not have been enough to make Earth scientists discard Wegener's theory entirely. It was true, as Wegener himself admitted, that the causes for continental motion he chose were not very convincing. However, he and others have pointed out, there were many other times when scientists accepted the idea that something *had* happened—if the factual evidence was compelling enough—even when they had little or no understanding of how or why it had happened. For instance, as Naomi Oreskes writes in *The Rejection of Continental Drift*, geologists accepted that huge folding or overthrusts had taken place in the Alps, moving rocks for hundreds of miles, because the evidence that this had occurred was overwhelming—even though they had no idea how or why it had happened. Although most of the criticisms of Wegener's individual pieces of evidence (or his interpretation of them) were justified, they were not strong enough to destroy his whole theory, historians say. Why, then, was continental drift so violently rejected?

The fact that the feelings of the scientists at the New York meeting went beyond professional disagreement was shown in the language that many of them used. They mocked not only the continental drift theory, but Wegener personally, in bitingly sarcastic comments. Pierre Termier, the director of the Geological Survey of France, damned Wegener with faint praise by saying that his hypothesis was "a beautiful dream, the dream of a great poet. One tries to embrace it, and finds that he has in his arms but a little vapor or smoke; it is at the same time both alluring and intangible." Rollin T. Chamberlin of the University of Chicago put his opinion more bluntly: "Wegener's hypothesis . . . is of the foot-loose type . . . that . . . takes considerable liberty with our globe and is less bound by restrictions or tied down by awkward, ugly facts than most of its rival theories." (A few commentators of the time were blunter still. The president of the American Philosophical Society called the drift theory "Utter, damned rot.")

The historians have debated why Wegener's theory aroused such powerful emotions. Part of the reason, some have said, was that Wegener was an outsider. He was not a geologist, a geophysicist, a paleontologist, or a geodesist—he was a meteorologist. Many Earth scientists felt that he had no right to comment on subjects outside his own field. For instance, Charles Schuchert said, "It is wrong for a stranger to the facts he handles to generalize from them to other generalizations." Perhaps Wladimir Köppen had feared this sort of reaction when, after Wegener had first described continental drift to him in 1912, he told his future son-in-law to stick to meteorology. The fact that Wegener was a national outsider as well—a German, with whose country the United States had been at war less than a decade earlier—may have added to American feelings against him.

Different Approaches to Science

More fundamentally, several historians say, criticisms of Wegener were stronger in the United States than in Europe because of basic disagreements about the best way to do science. "Arguments [about continental drift] were not just about facts but also theories, methods and aims," H. E. LeGrand writes in *Drifting Continents and Shifting Theories.* Europeans were comfortable with Wegener's approach of forming a tentative idea (working hypothesis) and then seeking out factual evidence to support it—the so-called deductive method. The fact that most of Wegener's evidence did not come from his own research also fitted within the European scientific tradition. Scientists in the United States, on the other hand, believed

Inductive and Deductive Reasoning

There are two commonly used methods of reasoning, or moving between facts and possible explanations for those facts. Scientists, like other humans, use both methods all the time. People often use the methods alternately, in a sort of cycle moving from the unknown to the known and back again.

Most commonly, scientists begin with inductive reasoning. Inductive reasoning travels from particular facts or observations to an explanation for those observations as a group. It moves from the specific to the general—what has been called a bottom up approach.

For instance, suppose that, for several days in a row, one notices that one's cats gather in the kitchen around 5:00 P.M.—whether one is in the kitchen at that time or not. This behavior forms a repeating pattern that one would like to explain. One remembers that one usually feeds the cats in the kitchen at about that hour, so one forms a hypothesis that the cats appear there because they expect to be fed.

A hypothesis is an educated guess based on what is known. It refers to specific facts and can be used to make predictions that can be tested. For instance, one's hypothesis about the cats might lead one to predict that if one changes one's pets' feeding time, one will also change the time that they arrive in the kitchen. One could test this prediction by feeding the cats at 6:00 P.M. for a week and strongly that the most important part of science was gathering data through one's own observations or experiments. Only after years of field or laboratory work, they thought, should a researcher offer a few tentative suggestions about the meaning of the facts that had been collected.

Edward Berry (1875–1945), a professor of paleontology at Johns Hopkins University who attended the New York meeting, summed up this kind of complaint about Wegener's scientific procedure in the following words:

> *My principal objection to the Wegener hypothesis rests on the author's method. This, in my opinion, is not scientific, but takes the familiar course of an initial idea, a selective search*

then seeing whether they continue to come to the kitchen at 5:00 or begin waiting until 6:00.

If the cats still appear at 5:00, one may need to modify the hypothesis (or perhaps continue observing in case the change takes longer than a week). If, on the other hand, one finds that the cats alter their behavior to fit with the new feeding schedule, the observations support the hypothesis. If one makes a similar set of tests with a dog and confirms the hypothesis that he goes to the front door at 8:00 A.M. each morning because he expects to be walked then, one might combine these hypotheses into the broader theory that cats and dogs can tell time. A theory is more general than a hypothesis and is supported by a wider collection of observations.

If one considers the theory to be well supported, one might then turn to deductive reasoning to explore this phenomenon further. Deductive reasoning starts with a general statement and moves to the specific—a top down approach. For example, starting with the theory that cats and dogs can tell time, one might form the hypothesis that if one rewards the cats or dog (say, with food or some activity that they enjoy) at a particular time and place each day, one will be able to train them to come to that place at that time. One can then design an experiment that will show whether this hypothesis holds true.

through the literature for corroborative evidence, ignoring most of the facts that are opposed to the idea, and ending in a state of auto-intoxication in which the subjective idea comes to be considered as an objective fact.

Wegener's ideas also brought up the old disagreements that had split geology in its youth as violently as mysterious forces had supposedly broken up Pangaea. One of these was the rivalry between catastrophism and uniformitarianism. Although Wegener did not actually describe any ancient catastrophes, many researchers felt that his theory implied them. Why else, they said, should Pangaea have broken up relatively suddenly in a geologically quiet time?

In some American minds, too, H. E. LeGrand speculates, Wegener's theory may have stirred up painful memories of the even deeper conflict between science and religion. Many scientists in the 19th century had associated catastrophism with belief in worldwide disasters described in the Bible, particularly Noah's Flood. Lyell's uniformitarianism, on the other hand, had come to be connected with Charles Darwin's theory of evolution, because both were based on the belief that "the present is the key to the past." The present seemed to echo the past just as much in the dispute between religion and science as it was supposed to do in geology: Just a year before the New York meeting, believers in a literal interpretation of the Bible had put a Tennessee high school biology teacher John Scopes (1900–70) on trial for violating a state law against teaching evolution. Wegener made no mention of religion in his writing, but some scientists may have feared that accepting any idea that resembled catastrophism might open the door to a renewed version of this larger conflict as well.

Starting All Over

Perhaps the deepest reason for Wegener's contemporary Earth scientists' violent rejection of continental drift, LeGrand and some other historians say, is that if Wegener's theory proved correct, it would destroy ideas that many of these scientists had spent their entire careers believing and studying. "We insist on testing this hypothesis with exceptional severity, for its acceptance would necessitate the discarding of theories held so long that they have become almost an integral part of our science," Chester Longwell said at the 1926 meeting. Or, as Rollin Chamberlin put it even more bluntly, "If we are to believe Wegener's hypothesis, we must forget everything which has been learned [about Earth science] in the last 70 years and start all over again."

Whatever the reasons for it, historians agree that the powerful disapproval of Wegener's hypothesis expressed at the New York meeting in 1926 seriously damaged further consideration of continental drift, especially in the United States, for many decades. Science historian Ursula B. Marvin writes in *Continental Drift: The Evolution of a Concept,* "Partly as a result of that symposium, more than 35 years were to pass before American geologists would meet again for the purpose of seriously discussing continental drift."

When Earth scientists' thoughts finally did turn back to his drift theory, Alfred Wegener was no longer alive to enjoy its revival.

Death on the Ice

5

After 1928, Alfred Wegener spent little time brooding about his fellow scientists' rejection of continental drift because he had something more exciting on his mind: a chance to return to Greenland. Johannes Georgi claimed in a memoir included in Schwarzbach's *Alfred Wegener* that the opportunity for this new expedition came through him.

Georgi by this time had established a successful meteorological career of his own with the Marine Observatory in Hamburg. In 1926 and 1927, while doing balloon studies in Iceland, he had discovered the powerful high-altitude wind currents called the jet stream. He wrote to Wegener in 1928, asking for advice about the possibility of setting up a weather balloon station on the Greenland ice cap to study these winds further. Wegener responded with enthusiasm, expanding Georgi's limited proposal into what Georgi called "a complete geophysical program."

The German economy was facing many difficulties, including massive inflation. Nonetheless, Georgi and Wegener persuaded the Emergency Aid Committee for German Science to promise funding for their expedition. Wegener explained that he planned for the trip to last a year and a half, during which expedition members would record daily air and ice temperatures and changes in the atmosphere at several locations. He hoped to establish a station on the ice cap itself and have men spend the winter there, which had never been done before. Among other things, they could measure the thickness of the ice cap by setting off explosions and measuring the waves that the explosions sent through the ice. They would use seismographs, the same tools used to measure natural earthquakes, to record the effects of these artificial ones. The expedition could also test new equipment for Arctic travel, such as motorized sledges.

The information his group gathered could help forecasters predict weather in northern Europe because that weather was strongly affected by the weather over Greenland, Wegener told the committee. The expedition's research would also benefit shipping in the North Atlantic, which was at risk from floating icebergs that came from the chilly island. It also might aid air travel between North America and Europe, still in the planning stages, because the planes' routes were likely to pass over Greenland.

Planning an Expedition

With the committee's support, Wegener, Georgi, and two other German scientists, Fritz Loewe (1895–1974) and Ernst Sorge (1899–1946), made a preliminary journey to Greenland in March 1929. Their chief task was to choose sites for the main expedition's two coastal base camps. The western camp needed to be near a spot on the interior ice sheet that was close to the shore and not too steep for dogs and sleds to climb. The group finally chose a location at the head of a fjord, or narrow inlet, called Kamarujuk, inside Umanak Bay. Wegener arranged with local Greenlanders to supply men, dogs, and dog food for the main expedition. The four men also made some preliminary scientific observations, including the first measurement of ice thickness using the seismic (explosion) method. They returned to Germany in November.

This photograph of Alfred Wegener's fellow polar explorers Johannes Georgi, Peter Freuchen, and Ernst Sorge (left to right) was taken just before Wegener's final expedition to Greenland in 1930–1931. Georgi, Sorge, and Fritz Loewe spent the winter on the Greenland ice cap at the expedition's Mid-Ice station. (ullstein bild/The Granger Collection)

Now came the work that might be harder than the expedition itself: choosing the scientists to go on the main expedition and gathering the many supplies that the group would need. The extensive packing list covered not only food for men and animals (the group planned to use both dogs and Icelandic ponies) but also kerosene fuel for heating and cooking, warm clothing, radios, and scientific instruments modified to function at subzero temperatures. It also included two propeller-driven motorized sledges, built to order by an airplane factory in Finland. Wegener hoped that these devices would travel faster and carry heavier loads than dogs, but they had never been tested under Arctic conditions.

Wegener, Georgi, and Sorge spent exhausting hours making lists, checking with suppliers, interviewing applicants, and arguing with the Emergency Committee and other agencies about funding. Through it all, Georgi wrote later, Wegener managed to retain his even temper and sense of humor, venting his frustrations only in the pages of the diary he kept. "His extraordinary calmness, his willingness to make sacrifices for the sake of his work, his affability, and his sense of fairness made him an ideal expedition leader," Wegener's father-in-law, Wladimir Köppen, wrote of him.

A Frustrating Start

At last, all the goods and equipment—amounting to 98 tons of material, packed into 2,500 crates, boxes, bags, and barrels—were assembled at Copenhagen and loaded onto the large Danish ship *Disko.* Wegener and the 13 other scientists said good-bye to their tearful families and departed on April 1, 1930. They stopped at Reykjavik, Iceland, 10 days later to collect 25 Icelandic ponies and three men to manage them. They then went on to Greenland, where they landed on April 15. There they had to transfer their supplies to a smaller ship, the *Gustav Holm,* which could move more easily among the ice floes. Unfortunately, they found that most of the sea ice on the northwestern coast had not yet broken up, so they could not reach the fjord where they wanted to set up their first base, West Station. They had to unload onto the ice near Uvkusigsat, a settlement on a nearby fjord. The *Gustav Holm* left them there on May 10.

Wegener's expedition unloaded their supplies from this small ship, the Gustav Holm, *onto the ice in northwestern Greenland in early May 1930. Because the sea ice refused to break up on schedule, however, they could not move on to the spot where they wanted to establish West Station, their first base. This delay created hardship for the expedition and was indirectly responsible for Wegener's death.* (Archive/Alfred Wegener Institute)

And then they waited . . . and waited . . . and waited. For 38 days beyond the time they hoped to start for the head of the fjord, Wegener and his men could do nothing because the sea ice blocking their path refused to melt. Even attempts to blast the ice loose with dynamite did not help. This delay not only wasted food and other supplies but cut into the limited time that the group would have for establishing the Mid-Ice (*Eismitte*) station on the inner ice sheet before winter made travel impossible. "Our expedition's program is slowly being seriously jeopardized by the obstinacy of the ice," Wegener wrote in his journal on June 9.

The ice finally broke up on June 17, letting the men begin at last to haul their supplies up the Kamarujuk fjord in their tiny motor-boat, the *Krabbe.* They then faced the task of dragging the boxes and bales up the steep side of the glacier to the nunatak, or stretch of rocky, ice-free ground, where they planned to set up West Station. They spent days—or rather, nights, lit by the glow of the summer's midnight Sun—chipping a path out of the ice for the load-carrying ponies to use. Dogsleds transported the material over sections of the glacier that were too steep for the ponies. The hardest work was bringing up the two motor sledges, which were too heavy for either dogs or ponies. They had to be dragged up the steepest part of the glacier by hand-operated winches and cables.

Meanwhile, Walthar Kopp and the two other scientists who were to establish the East Station left Copenhagen on July 10 and arrived at the mouth of Scoresby Sound on July 19. They had to wait even longer than the group in the west for the sea ice to melt and let them proceed to their destination. They reached the East Station site only on September 18, but they had their huts and weather station, including facilities for launching tethered balloons, completed by October 1, just in time for the first snowstorm of winter. They established radio contact with West Station for the first time on November 28.

Setting up Mid-Ice

Setting up West Station was only the beginning. Wegener's men still had to establish the Mid-Ice station, 250 miles (400 km) farther inland, in the center of the ice cap itself. The first trip from West Station to the site of Mid-Ice began on July 15, much later than Wegener had hoped. The motor sledges were still being assembled and tested, so dogs had to do the work.

Each round trip between West Station and Mid-Ice was expected to take a minimum of three weeks. Wegener calculated that transporting the 7,000 pounds (3,200 kg) of food, kerosene, and other supplies that the inner station needed would take at least six such trips with their present number of dogs and sleds. They would not have time to make that many journeys before winter, so they would have to hire more dogsled teams from the local Greenlanders.

Not surprisingly, the first journey across the ice cap was a great challenge. Johannes Georgi, who would be the chief scientist at Mid-Ice, led the trip. Two other scientists, Fritz Loewe and Karl Weiken, and eight Greenlanders went with him. As they moved inland, the men set up caches of food, kerosene, and other essential supplies for groups traveling between West Station and Mid-Ice to draw upon. They marked the path by placing a black flag on a pole every third of a mile (500 m) and building a cairn, or stack of rocks and snow, every three miles (5 km). These landmarks could be lifesavers in a blizzard, when straying from the trail would mean certain death.

The men and dogs had to climb from an altitude of 3,000 feet (915 m) at West Station to 9,850 feet (3,003 m) at Mid-Ice, and the decrease in oxygen as they ascended made them tire easily. The Greenlanders grew nervous about remaining on the forbidding ice cap, where they did not usually travel, and began insisting on returning to the shore. Finally, at the halfway point, Loewe agreed to go back with five of the Greenlanders, leaving only three to go on with Georgi and Weiken. Fewer people meant fewer sleds, so much of the equipment intended for Mid-Ice had to be left at that spot.

The five men finally reached the Mid-Ice site on July 30. After unloading the limited supplies they had brought, all except Georgi headed back to West Station the following day. Georgi remained at Mid-Ice to set up the station and begin recording weather data. He emerged from his tent each morning to measure temperature, wind, humidity, and atmospheric pressure. During the day he tinkered with the instruments he had brought, trying to persuade them to function at the temperatures he found on the ice cap, which could drop to -20°F (-29°C) at night. He also dug a chamber in the ice to provide better shelter for himself and his instruments than the tent.

By the end of August, Wegener's men had hauled all the expedition's supplies up the glacier to West Station and made a second trip to Mid-Ice. Summer was nearly over, however, and Mid-Ice was still far from self-sufficient. "I'm afraid, really afraid, that we're not going to make it," Wegener had written in his journal as early as August 6.

The motorized sledges proved to be a great disappointment. Dubbed *Polar Bear (Eisbär)* and *Snow Sparrow (Schneespatz)*, they were finally ready for testing on August 29. The group found that the sledges' motors were too weak to haul heavy loads except in the best of weather, and even then they moved more slowly than Wegener had hoped. The temperamental devices could not handle steep slopes, opposing winds, wet snow, or unusually low temperatures.

A third dogsled party reached Mid-Ice on September 13. Georgi, now accompanied by Ernst Sorge, was well settled in, but the two men still needed more fuel, food, and explosives for their ice depth measurements. Georgi sent back a letter to Wegener with the returning sleds, saying that if they did not receive another shipment by October 20, he and Sorge would try to return to West Station because they would not have enough supplies at Mid-Ice to survive the winter.

Meanwhile, a crew attempting to bring the loaded motor sledges to Mid-Ice had left West Station a few days after the dogsled group. The motor team met the returning sled team at the halfway marker on September 17. To add to the motor crew's troubles, winter seemed to be starting early, and one storm after another slowed their progress. After a week, they finally had to admit that the sledges would never reach Mid-Ice. They turned back, only to have the engines of both sledges overheat. The men left the useless vehicles in the snow and traveled the rest of the way on foot, finally arriving on September 27.

Journeys to the Wegener expedition's Mid-Ice station had to use dogsleds like these. Wegener had brought two motorized sledges that were supposed to be able to carry large loads, but they refused to function properly in the ice cap's challenging environment. (The Granger Collection)

International Polar Year: A Modern Polar Adventure

Scientists today are just as drawn to the lands around the Earth's poles—the Arctic and Antarctic—as Alfred Wegener was. "We now know that these areas hold some of the keys that wind the world," Martin Varley wrote in the March 2007 issue of *Geographical,* the official magazine of Britain's Royal Geographical Society. Today, the subject of much of these scientists' research is an issue that Wegener never heard of: global warming.

One of the largest polar ventures of the early 21st century is the International Polar Year (IPY), a program organized by the International Council for Science and the World Meteorological Organization. IPY involves 211 projects, staffed by more than 50,000 scientists and support people from many fields and more than 60 countries. The program runs from March 2007 to March 2009. Its projects focus on eight topic areas: Earth, land, people, ocean, ice, atmosphere, space, and education.

One of IPY's greatest concerns is the changes in snow and ice that have been reported in connection with global warming. If ice sheets such as the one covering Greenland were to melt, the extra water could raise sea levels enough to threaten coastal cities and low-lying areas around the world. At the same time, decreases in snowfall and shrinking of glaciers could cause shortages of freshwater. More than half of IPY's projects are related to global warming and related climate changes.

IPY researchers also hope to advance basic science, just as Alfred Wegener did. They seek clues to Earth's past climates that may be buried in ice cores, for instance. The Greenland ice sheet is one of the areas that will be cored. Another project will combine data from satellite radar and multi-beam sonar scanners carried beneath ships to study past and present changes in the deep seafloor. Some of these changes are related to the movement of the planet's landmasses.

IPY scientists draw on equipment that Alfred Wegener could hardly have imagined. In addition to satellites and sonar, they have fleets of icebreaker ships and automated gliders that carry instruments, for instance. At the same time, they use traditional Arctic exploration gear that Wegener knew well, such as dogs and sleds. Although modern communication and the possibility of quick air rescue make IPY scientists far safer than Wegener and his men were, they must still experience the isolation, danger, and beauty that characterize these forbidding lands.

Visiting Mid-Ice

As they neared West Station, the unhappy motor team, in turn, met Wegener and Fritz Loewe, who were leading a fourth dogsled trip to Mid-Ice with 13 Greenlanders and 15 sleds. Even before Wegener had seen Georgi's letter, he had decided that a final supply run to Mid-Ice was essential. He knew it would need to set out as soon as possible, before winter blocked the path completely. His team had left West Station on September 22, the day after the third party brought back the sleds and dogs they needed. Now, after hearing the sad story of the motor sledges, Wegener's group cached some of the supplies they had been carrying and instead packed up the most important items that had been in the sledge loads.

They did not get far. The Greenlanders in Wegener's party were used to chilly weather, of course, but their reindeer-skin clothing was not warm enough to keep out the degree of cold they now faced. They therefore insisted on turning back. Even Wegener's personal appeal and a promise of higher pay persuaded only four to remain, reducing the group to six sleds. After caching many items and repacking the rest, the tiny band continued on to Mid-Ice on September 29. They carried only about 4,000 pounds (1,800 kg) of supplies, far less than they had hoped.

As the days wore on, bad weather made three of the four remaining Greenlanders abandon the journey. Only one, a young man named Rasmus Villumsen, was willing to continue with Wegener and Loewe. The load for Mid-Ice therefore

Alfred Wegener's honesty, loyalty, and sense of fairness made the members of his expedition respect him as a leader. Wegener, in turn, was devoted to the expedition and its scientific work. He saw that work as a "sacred trust," worthy of "the greatest sacrifices." He ultimately sacrificed his life to its success. (Archive/Alfred Wegener Institute)

had to be cut yet again as the six sleds became three. Georgi's deadline passed, and Wegener had to hope that, if Georgi and Sorge had indeed left Mid-Ice, the two groups would meet on the trail. Continual blizzards and lack of food sapped the strength of men and dogs, and some of the weaker dogs had to be killed to make food for the rest. To add to their problems, Loewe told Wegener that his toes had become numb, a sign of frostbite. Wegener massaged Loewe's feet every night and morning in camp, hoping to restore circulation to them before the frozen flesh died and began to decay, but his efforts failed.

Wegener, Loewe, and Villumsen finally reached Mid-Ice on October 30. The temperature outside was down to -62°F (-52°C). They were thrilled to find that the station was not deserted: Georgi and Sorge, equally delighted to hear the sound of their sleds, rushed out of the ice cave in their underwear to greet them. As Georgi explained, he had concluded that trying to reach West Station on foot through the winter storms would be more risky than staying where they were, so the two had decided not to leave after all. He was bitterly disappointed at how little the men had been able to bring. Still, he calculated that if he and Sorge were very careful they might have enough fuel and food to see them through the winter.

Wegener, on the other hand, was excited to see how much Georgi and Sorge had accomplished. "You are comfortable here! You are comfortable!" he kept exclaiming. The ice cave, which the two men had completed on October 5, was a mere 23°F (-5°C) inside, cozy compared with the outside temperature. Lit by daylight that the icy roof filtered to a dim blue, the cave included a relatively large room (10 by 16 feet, or 3 by 5 m) with sleeping ledges and several smaller rooms for storage and other functions. The station also had an observation tower that reached 10 feet (3 m) above the surface.

Wegener was thrilled that Georgi and Sorge had decided to continue their scientific work at Mid-Ice through the winter in spite of the difficulties that their limited supplies would cause. Georgi later remembered him saying, "The fact that you [will] have spent the winter here in the middle of Greenland, even without any particular

Johannes Georgi and Ernst Sorge (later joined by Fritz Loewe) made themselves relatively comfortable at the expedition's Mid-Ice (Eismitte) station, shown here. The entrance to the station is left of center. In the center is the tower, made of blocks of ice. The wooden structure on the right contained weather instruments. To keep warm, the men spent much of their time in a cave hollowed into the ice. (Archive/Alfred Wegener Institute)

results in research, doing only the simplest and most routine measuring, is . . . worth all that has gone into the expedition."

Final Journey

The men quickly realized that their provisions, scanty as they already were for two, would have to stretch to cover three: Fritz Loewe could not possibly make the return journey on his frostbitten feet. Almost all of Loewe's toes had already turned black with gangrene. If they were not amputated soon, the infection in the dying tissue could spread into the rest of his feet or even his whole body. Georgi finally cut off Loewe's toes with a pocket knife in mid-November. As he wrote later, he had to manage the operation with "no knowledge of medicine, no book with instructions for this kind of problem, no surgical instruments, no anesthetic, [and] a minimal supply of bandages and disinfectant." Fortunately, the same cold that had cost Loewe his toes in the first place helped to keep the gangrene from spreading, and his wounds healed cleanly.

This photo of Alfred Wegener and Greenlander Rasmus Villumsen was taken at Mid-Ice on November 1, 1930, Wegener's 50th birthday, just before the two men left the station to attempt to return to the West Station. Wegener died about a day later, probably from a heart attack. Villumsen buried his leader's body and continued on; his own body was never found. (Archive/Alfred Wegener Institute)

Mid-Ice's supplies could not possibly support five people, so the group agreed that Wegener and Villumsen would have to chance returning to West Station. In order to survive on what they could carry, they planned to begin with two sleds but then kill dogs as they weakened and use them as food. When they had dogs enough for only one sled, Villumsen would drive the sled and Wegener would follow behind on his skis.

After celebrating Wegener's 50th birthday with some dried fruit and chocolate that they had saved for a special occasion, the men parted on November 1. As Georgi, Sorge, and Loewe waved good-bye to the two departing dogsleds, Georgi was comforted by the fact that, although Wegener was no longer in his youth, he was in excellent physical condition. He seemed almost as strong as the younger Villumsen. Villumsen, for his part, had grown into an experienced and courageous Arctic traveler. If anyone could make this perilous journey successfully, it would surely be these two. The weather, too, seemed promising. Still, Georgi wrote later, he was worried enough about his friend that "after the two sleds disappeared into the fog, I retired to the barometer room to compose myself."

He was right to worry. No one ever saw the two men alive again.

A Long Winter

Cut off from all outside communication (a radio was one of the many items destined for Mid-Ice that had been abandoned along the way), the three men at Mid-Ice endured the winter as best they could. They spent as much time as possible in their sleeping bags in order to keep warm and save fuel. Their usual meals were bread and oat porridge in the morning and canned or dried meat in the evening, with treats such as frozen whale meat and an apple or orange on special occasions. Each day they made their measurements, adjusted and repaired their instruments, took and developed photographs, and fought off the depression of the endless winter night. Sometimes, at least, the depression was offset by beauty, as Georgi wrote:

> *An hour ago I took a walk outside. The full moon in the eastern*
> *sky, burnished silver, seeming to smile scornfully at the northern*

lights which cast several broad curves from east to south, but whose pale light was faint compared to the moonshine.

As I walked along in -55° Celsius [-63° Fahrenheit] the surface of the snow groaned and creaked with every step, and now and again the sharp sound of a little snowquake caused by the walking—the subsidence of the uppermost strata of the snow—was audible far around. My breath formed thick clouds. . . . The whole effect was indescribable. Nature here is so completely alone, and pays no attention to us tiny intruders.

Life at West Station was less grim but in some ways even more depressing. Several of the men there went out to look for Wegener and Loewe in mid-November, just as the winterlong Arctic night was

---

A Memorial to Wegener: The Alfred Wegener Institute

Alfred Wegener was honored in several ways after his death. The city of Graz, for instance, changed the name of Blumengasse (Flower Way), the street on which the Wegener family had lived, to Wegener-gasse. The International Astronomical Union named a crater on the dark side of the Moon after Wegener in 1970. The memorial that probably would have pleased Wegener the most, however, is the Alfred Wegener Institute, located in Bremerhaven, Germany. Founded in 1980, the institute carries out polar and oceanic research in the Arctic and Antarctic as well as in temperate latitudes. The German ministry of education and research provides most of its funding.

One of the Wegener Institute's missions is to improve under-standing of interactions among the oceans, ice, and the atmo-sphere. It also works to improve knowledge of the animals and plants of the Arctic and Antarctic and to learn more about the way the polar continents and seas have evolved over time. One focus of its research today is the role that the polar regions play in the world's climate, especially in relation to global warming. The institute carries out some of its studies on its research ship, the *Polarstern* (Pole Star). The institute also has an archive of photographs and other material related to Alfred Wegener's life and work, especially his expeditions to Greenland.

beginning, but they found no sign of them and finally had to return to the station on December 5. They clung to the hope that all the men had simply remained at Mid-Ice for the winter. As spring came without any word, however, they became more and more sure that the worst had happened.

Grim Discovery

West Station could not send another expedition to Mid-Ice until April 23, 1931. On its way across the glacier, about halfway to Mid-Ice, the team passed a disturbing sight: Wegener's skis and ski pole, carefully upended and standing like sentinels in the snow. Anxious to go on, the group did not investigate further at that time.

A second group manning the motor sledges, now functional once more, caught up with the dogsled party around May 5 and then passed them, arriving at Mid-Ice on May 7. After the first enthusiastic greetings, Kraus (the leader of the rescue expedition) and Ernst Sorge blurted out at the same time, "Where's Wegener?" In the ensuing silence, both men knew what the answer had to be. Kraus, who had brought a radio, sent the sad news to Godhavn, a large Greenland settlement. Godhavn, in turn, relayed it to Germany.

Georgi remained behind at Mid-Ice, where he planned to continue making weather recordings until midsummer so that the expedition would have a full year of measurements on the ice cap. Loewe, still in poor health, returned to West Station with the motor sledge party. Sorge and the dogsled team, meanwhile, returned to the upended skis, the meaning of which they now guessed.

On May 8, digging below the skis, the group found Wegener's body buried in the ice. He had been carefully wrapped in two sleeping bag covers and laid on a sleeping bag and a reindeer skin. Karl Weiken, a member of the party, wrote that Wegener's face appeared "relaxed, peaceful, almost smiling" and "looked more youthful than it had before." Signs on the body suggested that Wegener had not frozen or starved but had died quietly in his tent, probably from a heart attack brought on by overexertion. Clearly Rasmus Villumsen had still been with him when he died and had done everything he could to bury the expedition leader with the respect he deserved.

The expedition members marked Wegener's grave with a crude cross made from his broken ski pole. Wegener's brother, Kurt, later erected a larger cross, but all signs of Wegener's grave and its markers have long since vanished beneath the ice. (Archive/Alfred Wegener Institute)

"It was touching to see the care with which [Villumsen] had buried Wegener; and one had to admire the pains he had taken to dig and mark the grave," Weiken wrote. The men returned Wegener's body to its icy grave and marked it with a large cairn of ice blocks, a cross made from Wegener's broken ski pole, and a black flag.

The last volume of the diary Wegener always kept and certain other personal effects were not with his body. The team concluded that Rasmus Villumsen must have taken them with him and pushed on in an attempt to reach West Station. They searched diligently for the Inuit's body and found several places where he had camped. Villumsen and the documents he carried, however, were never found.

Like Georgi at Mid-Ice, the men at West Station remained at their posts, continuing the work that they had come to accomplish. (The East Station crew had already finished their tasks and closed up

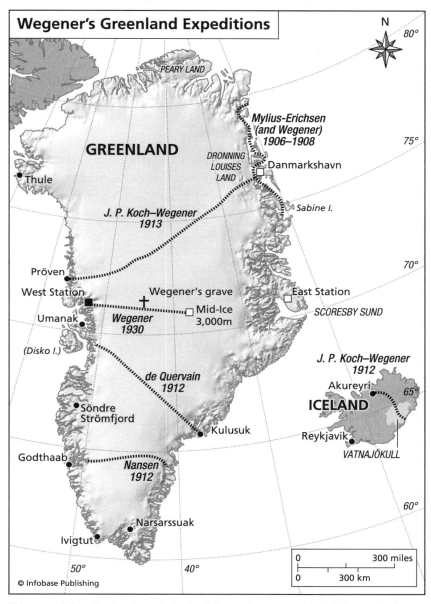

Wegener's Greenland Expeditions

N
80°

PEARY LAND

*Mylius-Erichsen
(and Wegener)
1906–1908*

75°

GREENLAND

DRONNING
LOUISES
LAND

☐ Danmarkshavn

• Thule

*J. P. Koch–Wegener
1913*

Sabine I.

70°

Pröven

West Station

Wegener's grave

☐ East Station

■

☐ Mid-Ice
3,000m

SCORESBY SUND

Umanak •

*Wegener
1930*

(Disko I.)

*de Quervain
1912*

*J. P. Koch–Wegener
1912*

Akureyri •

65°

• Söndre
Strömfjord

ICELAND

• Kulusuk

Reykjavik •

Godthaab •

*Nansen
1912*

VATNAJÖKULL

60°

• Narsarssuak

Ivigtut •

50°   40°

0   300 miles
0   300 km

© Infobase Publishing

*This map of Greenland and nearby Iceland shows the routes of Alfred Wegener's three
expeditions, as well as those of a few of the chilly island's other explorers.*

the station on May 10.) They were sure that Alfred Wegener would have wanted it that way. As Wegener had written to Georgi when the expedition was being set up in 1930, "Whatever happens, the cause [of the expedition and its scientific work] must not suffer in any way. It is our sacred trust, it binds us together, it must go on under all circumstances, even with the greatest sacrifices. That is, if you like, my expedition religion."

Kurt Wegener arrived in July to take over the leadership of the expedition, as Alfred had arranged before the group's departure. With his help, the men collected Georgi from Mid-Ice on August 7, closed up West Station, and sailed for home shortly afterward. Before they left, Kurt arranged for a 20-foot (6-m) high cross to be made of iron rods and placed over Alfred's grave. Snow and ice covered over even this monument as the decades passed. Today, all signs of Wegener's last resting place have long since vanished beneath the ice.

6

Rumblings of Change

When word of Alfred Wegener's death reached Europe, he was honored as a pioneer meteorologist and Arctic explorer. Heinrich von Ficker, a scientific colleague, called him a "Viking of science" in a memorial essay, for instance. For several decades, however, Wegener's role as the father of continental drift theory—and the theory itself—were all but forgotten.

Nonetheless, even during the years of the worst attacks on it, Wegener's theory had a few influential friends in the Earth science community. They kept its memory alive during the 1930s, 1940s, and 1950s. They also made it more acceptable to their fellow scientists by finding more evidence to support it and making changes in the theory's weakest points.

New Mechanisms for Drift

Reginald A. Daly (1871–1957), a highly regarded geology professor at Harvard University, became convinced that the continents might have moved after a trip to South Africa in 1922. During this visit he saw the rock formations that Alfred Wegener had claimed were so similar to those in South America, and he began to believe that Wegener's ideas might have merit. (Although Wegener's book had not yet been translated into English, Daly knew about the ideas in it because English reviews of it had appeared.)

Daly described his thoughts on continental movement in *Our Mobile Earth,* a book published in 1926. He proposed a different mechanism for the movement than Wegener did. Daly thought that the layer beneath the Earth's solid crust was a glasslike material, rigid in response to short-term stresses but yielding when acted on by small, long-term ones. Borrowing words coined earlier by Yale geology professor Joseph Barrell (1869–1919), Daly called this lower layer the asthenosphere, or "sphere of weakness," and the upper layer the lithosphere, or "sphere of stone." (Both of these terms are still used, although they are defined somewhat differently from the way Barrell and Daly used them.) The lithosphere was heavier or denser than the asthenosphere, Daly said. When the contraction of the Earth produced breaks in the crust, therefore, gravity would pull blocks of lithosphere down into the softer layer. This shift could move other nearby parts of the crust as well. Daly believed that portions of the crust also might move horizontally because the Earth bulged at the equator and the polar regions and dipped in between. Gravity would make landmasses slide toward this depression.

In Britain, continental drift's greatest defender was Arthur Holmes (1890–1965), a professor of geology at the University of Durham and, later, Edinburgh University. Holmes was best known as one of the pioneers who had developed techniques for using radioactive decay to determine the age of the Earth. Holmes in fact rejected several aspects of Wegener's version of continental drift and the evidence Wegener had chosen to support it. He noted, however, that "proving Wegener to be wrong is by no means equivalent to disposing of continental drift."

Holmes's greatest contribution to drift theory was to suggest a possible force for moving the continents that geologists could not immediately reject: convection currents in the sima or mantle. (Two Austrian geologists, Otto Ampferer [1875–1947] and Robert Schwinner [1878–1953], had mentioned the possibility of such currents in the first decade of the century, but their ideas had not been widely accepted.) Holmes first wrote about this idea in the late 1920s, and Wegener cited Holmes's work in the 1929 edition of his own book. Holmes described his convection current theory more fully in "Radioactivity and Earth Movements," a 1930 article in the *Transactions of the Geological Society of Glasgow,* and in an influential textbook *Principles of Physical Geology,* which was first published in 1944.

According to Holmes, the breakdown of radioactive elements in the sima produced heat that radiated out through the relatively thin,

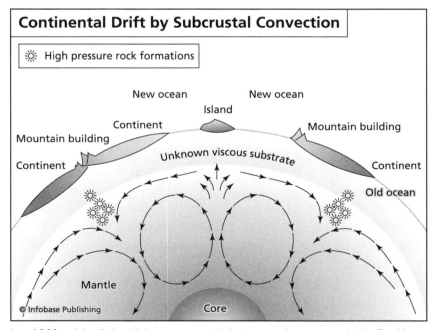

In a 1929 article, Arthur Holmes suggested that convection currents in the Earth's mantle might be able to move the continents in the way that Alfred Wegener had suggested. Harry Hess would later adapt some of Holmes's ideas in his own theory of seafloor spreading.

cold ocean floors but built up under the heavier continents. The temperature under the continents also was likely to be higher than under the ocean because the granite-type rocks that make up the continents contain more radioactive material than basalt-type ocean rocks. Because of these differences, convection currents would rise under the continents and sink under the ocean floors. At the spots where the currents rose and spread, they would push the crust apart and eventually tear it. As the currents turned downward, on the other hand, they would compress the edges of blocks of crust, creating high pressure and high temperature that turned the crust's rock into a denser type. Gravity would make this rock sink down into the mantle layer.

Holmes's emphasis on convection currents was not his only difference with Wegener's version of continental drift. Unlike Wegener, Holmes did not picture the continents ploughing actively through the sima like icebergs pushing through the sea. Rather, Holmes said that they simply rode along with the rest of the crust as the sima itself moved, carrying the crust with it. The Earth's rotation, he thought, would make upward-moving convection currents turn west and downward-moving currents turn east.

Support from South Africa

Drift's other greatest defender was South African geologist Alexander du Toit (1878–1948), whom Reginald Daly called "the world's greatest field geologist." Du Toit was an expert on the rocks of his native country, including the Karoo formation, whose similarities to rocks of the same age in other parts of the world had made Eduard Suess think of the protocontinent Gondwanaland. Wegener cited these similarities as a major support for his theory in later editions of his book.

After seeing the Karoo formation and meeting du Toit in 1922, Reginald Daly and Frederick E. Wright (1877–1953), a geologist at the Carnegie Institution of Washington, proposed that the institution send du Toit to South America to examine the formations that Wegener had claimed were so much like the South African ones. Du

Toit spent five months in Brazil, Uruguay, and Argentina in 1923 and found the similarities just as great as Wegener had said. He described his South American trip in a 1927 book called *A Geological Comparison of South America with South Africa.* In this book, he wrote of rocks he had seen in Brazil

> *Anyone who knows southern Africa will find the geology of this landscape startling. At every step I was reminded of the formations of Namaland and the Transvaal [parts of South Africa]. The Brazilian strata [layers of sedimentary rock] correspond perfectly in every detail to the strata series of the southern African shield.*

Du Toit was one of the most outspoken supporters of the continental drift theory after Wegener's death, although he did not describe it in quite the same way that Wegener had. For instance, instead of a single protocontinent, Pangaea, du Toit proposed two: Laurasia in the Northern Hemisphere and Gondwanaland in the Southern. Du Toit described his version of drift most fully in *Our Wandering Continents: An Hypothesis of Continental Drifting,* which appeared in 1937. Like Holmes, du Toit believed that convection currents in the mantle, produced by the heat that radioactive decay generated, moved the slabs of crust on which the continents rode.

In *A Revolution in the Earth Sciences,* an account of the continental drift controversy, science historian Anthony Hallam wrote, "Du Toit unquestionably made a substantial contribution to the drift hypothesis, partly by eliminating some of Wegener's errors and partly by integrating a vast amount of evidence, much of it new, into a plausible story whereby a wide array of disparate facts was given a coherent, simple interpretation." Unfortunately for drift theory, however, du Toit, like Wegener, did not pretend to be an objective reporter. He defended the theory in a writing style even more passionate than Wegener's and just as full of sarcasm as those of the critical scientists at the 1926 symposium. Even though du Toit's colleagues respected his geological fieldwork, many of them thought his writings about drift were too emotional to be truly scientific.

Comic Relief

The writings of Daly, Holmes, and du Toit improved some Earth scientists' opinions of continental drift in the 1930s and beyond, but many of those who had criticized the theory in the 1920s still rejected it. In 1944, for instance, Bailey Willis, who had objected to Wegener's ideas at the 1926 New York meeting, called the drift theory a "fairy tale."

Willis proposed a new version of the land-bridge idea in 1932 as an alternative to drift. He suggested that mountain-building forces beneath the ocean basins deform not only continental borders but the basins themselves, producing the mid-ocean ridges. These undersea mountain ranges continue onto the continents, from time to time forming what Willis called "isthmian links" between them. Ursula Marvin writes in *Continental Drift: The Evolution of a Concept*, "To many scientists Willis' isthmian links were the perfect compromise between the doctrine of permanence and the Suessian idea of submerged continents. . . . They seemed to remove all need for continental drift." Willis's theory became very popular in the 1930s, 1940s, and 1950s, especially in the United States.

Interest in the drift theory also remained low because evidence against it continued to emerge. For instance, new measurements by a group of British and Danish scientists in 1936 showed that the earlier determinations of longitude in Greenland, which had impressed Wegener so much, were in error. The revised figures showed no sign that the island was moving west, as Wegener had claimed.

Continental drift was not completely forgotten during this period. Most geology textbooks described it, at least briefly, as one of a number of theories about what might have happened to the Earth's crust during past geological eras. Professors mentioned it in their college classes, too, but often only as comic relief. For instance, Percy E. Raymond, a professor of paleontology at Harvard, liked to tell his students that half of a fossil sea creature had been found in Newfoundland and another half in Ireland. The two parts matched so perfectly, Raymond said, that they had to belong to the same animal, which had been "wrenched apart by Wegener's hypothesis in the late Pleistocene." When scientists considered drift at all, they thought of it in the revised versions offered by researchers like Holmes, not in the form in which Wegener had originally presented it.

Dragging Gravity

While most Earth scientists were ignoring or making fun of continental drift, a few were making discoveries that would bring attention back to this half-forgotten theory. Most of these findings were from the deep sea, a part of the Earth about which scientists knew next to nothing in Wegener's day. A few oceanic research expeditions, such as the ones carried on the British ship *Challenger* in 1872 and the German ship *Meteor* in the mid–1920s, had dropped dredging buckets down to bring up samples of material from different parts of the ocean floors. They had also conducted soundings, or depth measurements, with weights lowered on the ends of ropes. The information that could be revealed in these ways, however, was very limited.

Some of the new discoveries came from measurements of gravity, the same kind of study that had led to the theory of isostasy. By the early 20th century, researchers could measure local gravitational fields with a device called a gravimeter, which was far more accurate and easier to use than George Everest's plumb bob.

Dutch geophysicist Felix A. Vening Meinesz (1887–1966) invented a gravimeter that could be used at sea and tested it on a Dutch submarine in the Pacific Ocean near Indonesia in 1923. He found lower-than-normal gravity values over the deep-sea trenches in the area. This could mean, he said, that convection currents at these spots were dragging lightweight oceanic crust down into the denser layer below.

Vening Meinesz's measurements were one of the first signs that parts of the Earth's crust not only might have moved in the distant geological past but were still moving in the present day. He found similar results in an expedition to the Caribbean and Gulf of Mexico in 1928 and in returns to Indonesia in 1932 and 1936. His findings suggested that the seafloor crust near the trenches was being squeezed or compressed horizontally, perhaps because two convection cells (circles of rising and falling currents) were colliding there.

This stress, Vening Meinesz and his coworkers thought, had created the Indonesian islands and was responsible for the earthquakes and volcanoes so common in the region. Their results suggested that the crust under the oceans was fairly strong, but the layer beneath it was weak. This pattern fitted better with the Airy model of isostasy—the one Alfred Wegener preferred—than with the Pratt model.

Artificial Earthquakes

Researchers in the 1930s also began applying to the deep sea the same technique by which Wegener's 1930 expedition had measured the thickness of Greenland's ice: setting off explosions to create artificial earthquakes and measuring the resulting shock waves with seismographs. Scientists dropped explosive charges from ships, then

William Maurice ("Doc") Ewing was an expert on undersea echo sounding and seismology. He founded the Lamont Earth Observatory for Columbia University in 1949. Unlike some other Lamont researchers, he resisted the idea that the continental drift theory might be true until the evidence became overwhelming in the mid-1960s.
(AIP Emilio Segrè Visual Archives)

detected the echoes of the blasts with hydrophones. The powerful sound waves from the explosions went through the ocean floor and bounced off the rock layers beneath, allowing researchers to measure the thickness of the crust and the sediment that covered it. This seismic technique also helped them find out what kinds of rocks made up the crust at particular spots.

Maurice Ewing (1906–74), then at Lehigh University in Bethlehem, Pennsylvania, pioneered undersea seismology in the 1930s. He found, as Wegener had suggested, that the layer of continent-like, or sialic, rocks on the ocean floor was very thin. In some places it did not appear to exist at all. Most of the ocean floor, instead, was made of basalt-type rocks. The crust on the seafloor was only about 3.7 miles (6 km) thick, whereas the continental crust was more than 24.9 miles (40 km) thick. Ewing also discovered that the layer of sediment over the seafloor rocks was much thinner than expected. This suggested that the ocean floors were young—200 million years old or less. Evidence from fossils and radioactive dating of rocks confirmed this result.

War Spurs Marine Science

Because of submarine warfare, the navies of several countries, especially the United States, became very interested in the deep sea during World War II. Their interest continued in the 1950s during the cold war, an intense rivalry between the United States and the Soviet Union. The result was a tremendous upswing in deep-sea research and technology. In the United States, the navy's Office of Naval Research, founded in 1946, and the federal government's National Science Foundation, founded in 1950, paid for most of these marine science projects. Three academic facilities carried out the bulk of them: the University of California's Scripps Institution of Oceanography in La Jolla; the Woods Hole Oceanographic Institution in Woods Hole, Massachusetts; and Columbia University's Lamont Geological Observatory (later Lamont-Doherty Earth Observatory, now part of the Earth Institute) in New York.

William Menard, a marine geologist at Scripps, described the explosion in knowledge of the deep sea during that era this way:

By 1956 Lamont, using Navy submarines, had tripled the number of gravity observations at sea. . . . There were perhaps 100 cores of sediment from deep-ocean basins in 1948. By 1956 Lamont had taken 1,195. . . . By 1962 Scripps had about

Scripps, Woods Hole, and Lamont: Three Pioneering Institutions

Of the three institutions that provided most of the research that changed scientists' views of the Earth's history, the Scripps Institution of Oceanography was founded first. Funded partly by the family of E. W. Scripps, a wealthy newspaper owner, it began as the Marine Biological Association of San Diego in 1903. It became part of the University of California in 1912 and was renamed the Scripps Institution for Biological Research. According to the Scripps Web site, it was the first permanent marine science facility in the Western Hemisphere. It took on its present name in 1925. Scripps research in the 1940s and 1950s included studies of sonar, the ecology of kelp (giant seaweed) beds, and the discovery of the Mid-Pacific Ridge, part of the mid-ocean ridge.

Woods Hole Oceanographic Institution, founded in 1930, is part of the Marine Biological Laboratory, which has existed in Woods Hole, Massachusetts, since 1888. Much of the money to build the institution came from the Rockefeller Foundation. It expanded greatly in the 1940s and 1950s and became a leader in oceanographic research on the East Coast, as Scripps was on the west. It did pioneering research in seismology, geophysics, and meteorology as applied to the oceans. The Office of Naval Research and, later, the National Science Foundation funded much of its research. Its fleet of research vessels has included the famous submersible *Alvin*.

The Lamont-Doherty Earth Observatory is part of Columbia University. Maurice Ewing founded it as the Lamont Geological Observatory in 1949 in a Hudson River mansion donated by the widow of Thomas W. Lamont, a New York banker. It was renamed the Lamont-Doherty Geological Observatory in 1969 and took its present name in 1993. Its specialty has been mapping the ocean floors, including studies of their gravity, magnetism, and seismology. It has huge collections of echo sounder and seismic tracings, cores, and dredge samples from the seafloor. It is also known for its analysis of undersea rocks and studies of ocean water and currents.

1,000. There had not been seismic stations in the deep sea, and by 1965 there were hundreds. . . . The number of deep-sea soundings had increased by about 10^8 [100,000,000 times] . . . . Nothing comparable to shipboard magnetic profiles had ever been known, [but then] Lamont and Scripps . . . towed magnetometers for hundreds of thousands of kilometers. . . . Even in 1964 I was only half jesting when I wrote of a "digression from the familiar ocean basins to the mysterious continents."

One of the devices used in the postwar marine science explosion, the echo sounder, had been used first in an earlier war: World War I. The sounder was developed in 1911 to help ships in the North Atlantic spot floating icebergs, but when the war began, the sounder was adapted to let ships detect enemy submarines instead. The device sent waves of sound down through the water and recorded the returning waves generated when the outgoing waves struck solid objects. (Bats use a form of natural echo sounder to guide them as they fly at night.) Analysis of the recorded echoes showed how far away the objects were and gave some idea of their composition.

During World War II, Maurice Ewing, the seismology expert, and J. Lamar Worzel (1919–   ) modified the echo sounder to produce continuous recordings that revealed the heights and depths of the seafloor. (Unlike seismology, which provided information about layers of rock far beneath the ocean floor, the echo sounder produced maps of the floor's surface.) The sounder sent out an electronic tone at regular intervals. A microphone inside the hull of the ship that carried the device picked up the echo of the tone, reflected from the ocean bottom, and recorded it with a stylus on a continuously spooling strip of paper. Ewing and other scientists expanded their echo sounding research after the war, accumulating thousands of miles' worth of tracings. Their results suggested that the ocean bottom could be divided into three regions: the continental shelves, the deep seafloor, and the undersea mountain ranges called mid-ocean ridges.

The Wound That Never Heals

Maurice Ewing did his wartime echo sounder research at Woods Hole, but he went on to join Columbia University in 1944. In 1949

With Marie Tharp, Bruce Heezen discovered that ranges of undersea mountains, split down their centers by rift valleys, curved through the middle of all the Earth's oceans. He called this mid-ocean ridge system "the wound that never heals." (Woods Hole Oceanographic Institution Archives)

he founded the university's Lamont Earth Observatory at a converted mansion in the Hudson River Valley in 1949. There he gave his seismic and echo sounding profiles to one of the institute's scientists, Bruce Heezen (1924–77), and suggested that Heezen use them to draw up a map of the ocean floor. Heezen in turn assigned the project to Marie Tharp (1920–2006), a young woman who had just been hired as a drafting assistant in his department. Tharp's father had been a cartographer, or mapmaker, so she was very familiar with maps. She was also one of the few women of her time who had a master's degree in geology; she had a degree in mathematics as well.

Laying out thousands of tracings from echo sounders and seis-mographs, Tharp began drawing up a map of the North Atlantic in 1952. The map's most prominent feature was the Mid-Atlantic Ridge, a chain of huge undersea mountains running north and south down the middle of the sea. Scientists had known about this ridge since the *Challenger* expedition in the 1870s. Tharp, however, noticed something different about it: It seemed in fact to be two ranges, side by side, with a narrow, V-shaped valley running between them. It reminded Tharp of the well-known Rift Valley in East Africa, which Alfred Wegener had suggested was a spot where continents were moving away from each other. When she first told Heezen about the undersea rift valley, though, he rejected it with a groan: "It can't be. It looks too much like continental drift!"

Tharp soon returned with new evidence for her seemingly out-rageous claim. A map of deep-sea earthquakes drawn up by another scientist in the same laboratory showed that the quakes were concen-trated along the same valley she had noticed. That match increased the odds that the valley was real—and important. After a year of discussions, Tharp finally convinced Heezen that she was right.

Tharp and Heezen went on to make maps of the world's other ocean basins. They found that the Mid-Atlantic Ridge—and its cen-tral rift valley—were not alone. Similar ranges of mountains and val-leys associated with undersea earthquakes appeared on the floor of every sea. Together they formed a gigantic chain some 40,000 miles (64,000 km) long that snaked around the Earth like the curving seam on a baseball. These undersea ranges blended into rift valleys on land in sites such as East Africa and the line of the San Andreas Fault in California. Heezen became convinced that the valleys represented a crack in the Earth's crust through which new crust was constantly being formed by volcanoes that spewed up hot lava from the mantle layer beneath. He called the curving line of interconnected gashes "the wound that never heals."

Maurice Ewing disliked the idea of continental drift even more than Heezen had. Nonetheless, Heezen in turn finally persuaded Ewing that he and Tharp had actually found evidence that supported Wegener's half-discarded theory. Ewing first described the global ridge-and-rift system at a meeting of the American Geophysical

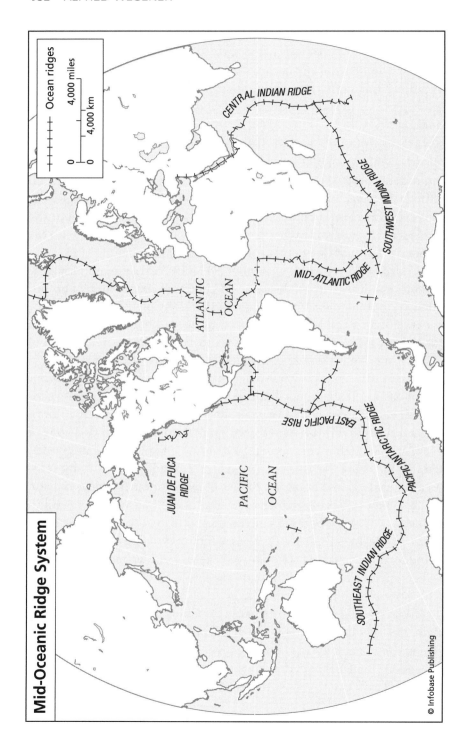

Mid-Oceanic Ridge System

Ocean ridges

4,000 miles

0

4,000 km

0

CENTRAL INDIAN RIDGE

SOUTHWEST INDIAN RIDGE

ATLANTIC OCEAN

MID-ATLANTIC RIDGE

EAST PACIFIC RISE

PACIFIC ANTARCTIC RIDGE

JUAN DE FUCA RIDGE

PACIFIC OCEAN

SOUTHEAST INDIAN RIDGE

Union in 1956, and Heezen did the same during another meeting at Princeton University in 1957. After this latter meeting, Harry Hess (1906–69), the head of the Princeton geology department, told Heezen, "Young man, you have shaken the foundations of geology."

Magnetic Moments

Some of the most important discoveries in the 1950s came from a geological specialty that had not even existed in Alfred Wegener's time: paleomagnetism, the study of the Earth's magnetic field in past geological eras. Scientists had known for hundreds of years that the planet acts like a giant magnet, producing its own magnetic field. It has north and south magnetic poles as well as geographical ones. They had also known that rocks containing large amounts of iron, such as basalt and some other kinds of igneous rocks—rocks made from the molten material of the mantle and spewed out in volcanoes or other eruptions from the depths—could be magnetized. The first compass needles, in fact, came from a naturally magnetized mineral called magnetite, or lodestone.

Igneous rocks pick up their magnetic alignment as they cool past a certain temperature, called the Curie point after French physicist Pierre Curie. The iron particles in the rocks align in the direction that the planet's magnetic field has at the time they pass this temperature, and they keep that alignment after the rocks harden. Some kinds of sedimentary rocks, made from material deposited on ancient seabeds, can be magnetized by a different process; they also keep their magnetic alignment. These magnetized rocks therefore become what marine archaeologist and explorer Robert Ballard has called "fossil compass needles." Comparing magnetized rocks of different ages (as determined by measuring radioactive decay in them) can reveal patterns of past changes in the planet's magnetic field.

In the mid-1950s, scientists studying paleomagnetism found that the Earth's magnetic poles (and therefore probably also the

(Opposite page) *In the mid-1950s, Marie Tharp, Bruce Heezen, and Maurice Ewing showed that a single, more or less continuous system of mountains (ridges) and narrow rift valleys, which they called the mid-ocean ridge, snakes through the floors of the world's oceans like the seam on a baseball. The ridge system proved to be a major site where new crust is created through seafloor spreading.*

geographic poles) appeared to have had different locations in the past. In other words, the poles had "wandered," more or less as Alfred Wegener had said. Stanley K. Runcorn (1922–95) and other geologists at Cambridge University in England announced in 1955 that, according to "fossil" magnetic fields in European rocks of different ages, the planet's magnetic north pole seemed to have changed its position steadily over geologic time. Runcorn believed that the pole had started from a spot near Hawaii in the Proterozoic eon and reached its present position in the Upper (later) Tertiary.

At first, Runcorn did not feel that his evidence for polar wandering necessarily supported continental drift. When his group went on to study rocks in North America, however, they found that rocks of the same age on the two continents showed *different* polar wandering paths. The only sensible explanation for this fact was that the continents had occupied different positions in earlier times than they do today. From 1956 on, therefore, Runcorn became a strong supporter of the drift theory. Other researchers found similar results in the rocks of the continents thought to have made up the former Gondwanaland.

At the same time Stanley Runcorn was finding magnetic evidence that the poles—or the continents, or both—had wandered in the past, two researchers at the Scripps Institution of Oceanography made a second important discovery in paleomagnetism. They used a new form of sensitive magnetometer—an instrument that can measure the strength and direction of a magnetic field—that P. M. S. Blackett (1897–1974), a British physicist, had invented shortly after World War I. During World War II, Blackett's magnetometer had been modified so that it could be towed behind aircraft or ships to detect enemy submarines. Scientists at Scripps improved the device further in the 1950s, making it able to create continuous recordings of the magnetic fields given off by rocks on the seafloor.

In 1955 and 1956, Scripps scientists Ronald Mason and Arthur Raff (1917–99) used shipborne magnetometers to obtain magnetic patterns around an undersea ridge (mountain range) in the northeastern Pacific, off North America's western coast. Their results were totally unlike any that had been found on land. In two different areas they found patterns of strongly and weakly magnetized rocks, alternating like the stripes on a bar code or a zebra's back. The stripes ran north and south, just like the ridge. They also were offset, or displaced relative to one another, along earthquake faults that ran perpendicular to the ridge.

Raff and Mason published their "zebra maps" in a paper in the August 1961 issue of the *Geological Society of America Bulletin.* At the time, the two scientists could not explain their results. Their findings, however, would be the first of a series that provided the key for understanding how the Earth creates new crust and, in the process, moves the continents.

The Plate Tectonics Revolution

7

A few years after Bruce Heezen's startling speech at Princeton, Harry Hess took his own turn at shaking the foundations of geology. He did so by turning from the land, geology's traditional place of study, to the sea.

In what he called "an essay in geopoetry," Hess offered a complete theory of the way the Earth's crust was formed, destroyed, and recycled beneath the oceans. He first described his ideas in a report to the Office of Naval Research in 1960. He circulated the report widely in manuscript form before finally publishing it as "History of the Ocean Basins" in an anthology of papers that appeared in 1962. Robert Dietz (1914–95), who worked for the Office of Naval Research, published a similar theory in 1961 and gave it the name by which both his and Hess's ideas generally became known: seafloor spreading.

Seafloor Spreading

The Earth's crust, Hess said, moved slowly but constantly. It was pushed and pulled by the same force that Arthur Holmes and a few others had spoken of for decades: convection currents in the asthenosphere, the soft, weak layer on which the crust rested. Unlike Holmes, however, Hess focused on the way these currents affected seafloors rather than landmasses.

Hess believed that rising convection currents forced the crust apart along the valley inside the mid-ocean ridge. As the crust tore open, hot water rushed upward into the gap. The water reacted with the crust's edges to create a new form of rock. (Dietz said instead that the new material was magma, or molten rock, that oozed up into the cracks from the mantle.

In 1962, Harry Hess of Princeton University published the theory of sea- floor spreading, which explains how the Earth's crust is created and destroyed on the ocean floors. Hess believed that the continents did not push through the mantle, as Alfred Wegener had proposed, but rather were carried along with the rest of the crust as convection currents in the mantle moved it. (Princeton University Library)

Earth scientists now believe that this view is correct.) Each wave of new rock pushed the older rock away from the crack on both sides. Because the new rock was hot, it was less dense than the rock it displaced. It therefore rose up and formed parallel ridges on both sides of the valley. The ridges sloped off on the outside as the rock cooled and sank to the level of the seafloor plain.

The motion of the crust that began at these spots slowly changed the location of the continents, carrying them along as if on a conveyor belt. This picture, Hess emphasized, was quite different from Alfred Wegener's proposal that the continents pushed through the mantle layer on their own. "The continents do not plow through oceanic crust impelled by unknown forces," Hess wrote in his 1962 paper.

"Rather they ride passively on mantle material as it comes to the surface at the crest of the ridge and then moves laterally away from it."

Bruce Heezen and some other scientists who shared Hess's belief that new ocean floor was created inside the mid-ocean ridges had thought that the Earth must be expanding to accommodate the new crust. Hess, however, said that crust was destroyed as well as created, leaving the planet's size unchanged. The destruction came in the ocean trenches, where the sinking side of convection cells pulled pieces of crust down into the hot asthenosphere and melted them. Hess had begun to suspect the role of the trenches after joining Felix Vening Meinesz on the 1930s expeditions that revealed unusually low gravity in oceanic trenches. Hess called the trenches the "jaw crushers" of his crust-recycling system.

Hess's theory was the first to describe a complete cycle for seafloor movement, covering both creation and destruction. It also

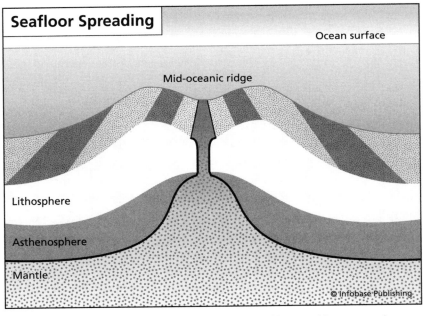

An illustration that shows how seafloor spreading at a mid-ocean ridge can create new crust. Molten rock from the Earth's mantle is forced upward to the surface of the crust at vents or fissures in the rift valley within the ridge. When the hot liquid rock contacts the icy ocean water, the rock solidifies, pushing away the seafloor on either side of it. As the seafloor moves away from the valley, it forms the mountains of the ridge.

explained Maurice Ewing's observation that the seafloor appeared to be very young—a mere 200 to 300 million years old at the most. At first, however, it did not shake the foundations of geology very hard, because Hess could provide little evidence to support it. Almost the only geological fact he cited was a discovery that he himself had made during World War II, when he had been captain of the *Cape Johnson,* a troop transport ship that repeatedly crossed the Pacific Ocean. The *Cape Johnson* had an echo sounder that was supposed to be used to show the depth of water off unknown coastlines so that the *Cape Johnson* would not run aground. Hess, however, left the sounder on all the time, even when the ship was in the open sea. The result was a continuous tracing of the heights and depths of the ocean floor.

The sounder had revealed isolated, flat-topped mountains lying on the seafloor between the mid-ocean ridges and the trenches, their tops far below the level of the waves. Hess called these strange seamounts guyots, after Arnold Henry Guyot (1807–84), Princeton's first professor of geology. He later concluded that the guyots were extinct volcanoes, formed as parts of the ocean ridges. Their tops had once projected above the water, but erosion had slowly flattened them down to sea level. As the moving crust pushed the guyots away from the peaks of the ridges, Hess wrote, they sank lower and lower, eventually reaching levels as much as 1.2 miles (2 km) below the water. Hess noticed that the farther away the guyots were from the mid-ocean ridge, the deeper (and therefore probably older) they were. In his 1962 essay he said that the changing position of the guyots provided evidence that the location of geological features in the ocean could change dramatically over time.

Linking Spreading to Magnetic Changes

About the time Hess was publishing his work, Frederick Vine (1939–   ), a geophysicist at Britain's Cambridge University, became interested in the underwater magnetic "bar codes" that Arthur Raff and Ronald Mason had observed a few years earlier. Vine made magnetometer tracings of his own during a 1962 cruise to the Carlsberg Ridge in the Indian Ocean and programmed a computer to turn them into a kind of map. He found a striped pattern much like the one Raff and Mason had seen. Vine and his adviser at Cambridge, Drummond Matthews (1931–97), wrote a paper on the subject, "Magnetic Anomalies over Oceanic Ridges," which appeared in the journal *Nature* in September 1963.

In their paper, Vine and Matthews connected the striped magnetic patterns with Hess's theory of seafloor spreading. They also linked these ideas with another subject that paleomagnetism researchers were investigating: possible past reversals in the Earth's magnetic field. The magnetism in most rocks is oriented toward the north magnetic pole; that is why lodestone compass needles pointed north. In the early 20th century, however, a French physicist Bernard Brunhes (1867–1910) and a Japanese geophysicist Motonori Matuyama (1884–1958) found magnetized rocks that were oriented toward the south pole instead. These discoveries led the men to propose that the Earth's magnetic field had reversed its polarity from time to time during past geological eras.

Most Earth scientists thought this idea too fantastic to consider, but some support for it had been found by the time Vine and Matthews wrote their paper. In the 1950s, researchers had developed an improved technique for dating rocks that was based on the breakdown of radioactive potassium into argon. Using this technique, two groups of paleomagnetists showed in the early 1960s that lava rocks of the same age from different parts of the world had the same magnetic polarity, whether normal or reversed. This fact supported the idea that the reversals in the rocks had come from changes in the Earth's whole magnetic field rather than from local effects.

Allan Cox (1926–87), Richard Doell (1923–2008), and Brent Dalrymple (1937–   ), three California geologists, proposed in the early 1960s that if a time line for past magnetic reversals could be worked out by means of radioactive dating, the reversals themselves could be used as a dating technique. They published the first crude time line of magnetic reversals in land rocks in 1963 and an improved version in 1964. The time line included four long "epochs," named after magnetic research pioneers, and numerous "events"—very brief reversals, lasting less than 100,000 years each—named after locations. Identification of the events allowed the dating to be very precise.

Vine and Matthews wrote that the magnetic striping they had seen was

> *consistent with, in fact virtually a corollary of, current ideas on ocean floor spreading and periodic reversals in the Earth's magnetic field. . . . If spreading of the ocean floor occurs, blocks of alternatively normal and reversely magnetized material would drift away from the centre of the [mid-ocean] ridge and parallel to the crest of it.*

The patterns of stripes on the left and right sides of a ridge would be mirror images of each other, Vine and Matthews said, because the rocks on both sides of the ridge were formed at the same time and place. The rocks therefore would cool and pick up their magnetization at the same time. As time passed and the Earth's magnetic field reversed, strips of normal and inverted polarity would be laid down. The mirror-image effect would remain because the layers of rock would be pushed away from the ridge at about the same speed in both directions.

Lawrence Morley (1920–   ), a Canadian geophysicist, developed a set of ideas much like those of Vine and Matthews at about the same time, so the proposal that seafloor spreading and magnetic seafloor striping explained each other became known as the Vine-Matthews-Morley hypothesis. At first it went over, David M. Lawrence quotes Vine as saying in *Upheaval from the Abyss: Ocean Floor Mapping and the Earth Science Revolution,* like "the classic lead balloon." Most Earth scientists rejected it because it combined three ideas that were all regarded as unproven at best: seafloor spreading, the past reversal of the Earth's magnetic field, and the possible use of "fossil" magnetism in rocks as a method of dating.

Vine and John Tuzo Wilson (1908–93), a geophysicist at the University of Toronto, tested the Vine-Matthews-Morley proposal by recording magnetic striping around the Juan de Fuca Ridge, an undersea ridge in the waters off the state of Washington and the coast of British Columbia. In a paper published in 1965, Vine and Wilson showed that in most places the striping revealed the symmetrical, mirror-image pattern they had predicted. They also used their theory and the Cox-Doell-Dalrymple chronology to create a computer model of the pattern that would be expected around the ridge if the seafloor had spread at a steady rate. The pattern produced by the model was fairly close to the pattern that Vine and Wilson had actu-

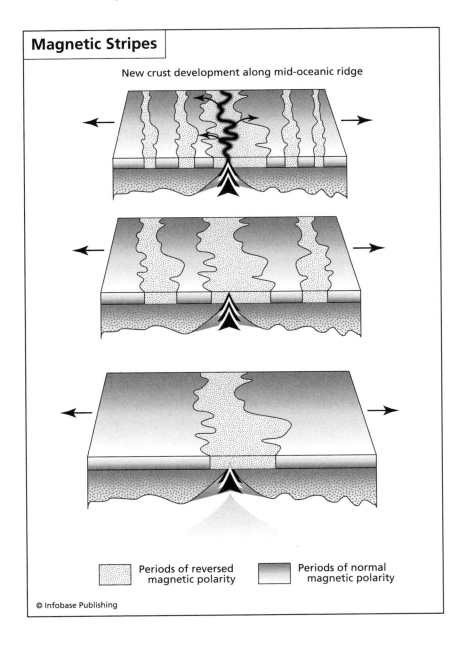

Magnetic Stripes

New crust development along mid-oceanic ridge

Periods of reversed magnetic polarity

Periods of normal magnetic polarity

ally found. When Vine changed the computer model to reflect some new dates in the magnetic time line that he learned about in late 1965, the model matched the real results even more.

Converging Lines of Evidence

Several researchers at Lamont Earth Observatory in New York, meanwhile, were also studying magnetic patterns in rocks. One, Neil Opdyke (1933–), examined layers of sedimentary rocks that other Lamont scientists had taken from the seafloor with coring devices. The patterns Opdyke and his students found in cores taken from several oceans showed a close match with both the striping patterns around the ridges and the time lines that Cox and his fellow workers had drawn up. The fact that Opdyke's sedimentary rocks and the Cox group's lavas showed the same pattern helped to confirm the idea that magnetic reversals were real and affected the Earth's entire magnetic field.

Opdyke and his graduate student John Foster also found good matches between dates for core layers obtained by the reversal method and those obtained by the more traditional technique of examining fossils in the core samples. This provided further confirmation that the reversal method was reliable. "Through magnetic reversals we can correlate synchronous events in different sediments, with different fossils, all over the world," William Wertenbaker quotes Opdyke as saying in *The Floor of the Sea.* In other words, as John Foster put it, the magnetic reversals were a "universal fossil."

A Lamont graduate student, Walter C. Pitman III (1931–), was working in the office next to Opdyke's. Pitman had sailed on a

---

(Opposite page) *Reversals of the Earth's magnetic field are recorded in the crust of the seafloor. When magma (molten rock) rises up from the mantle at a mid-ocean ridge and cools, iron crystals in the rock align with the direction (polarity) that the planet's magnetic field has at that time. Researchers found "stripes" of rocks showing normal and reversed magnetic fields, like a bar code or marks on a zebra's back, around several mid-ocean ridges. A timetable of magnetic reversals derived from land rocks, as well as dating of cores from the seafloor by use of fossils, confirmed that older pieces of crust were farther away from the ridges than younger ones. Some magnetic reversal patterns showed striking mirror-image symmetry centered on the ridges, suggesting that new crust was being pushed away from the ridges at an equal rate of speed on both sides.*

research vessel called the *Eltanin* in late 1965 when it made several passages through the waters of Antarctica, collecting a variety of oceanographic data. These data included magnetic profiles of the Pacific-Antarctic Ridge, part of the mid-ocean ridge system that Bruce Heezen and Marie Tharp had discovered. Pitman and another graduate student Ellen Herron began analyzing the profiles, along with some from an earlier cruise, when they returned to Lamont in November 1965. In December, Pitman noticed that the profiles from the part of the cruise labeled Leg 20 looked remarkably like Vine and Wilson's Juan de Fuca patterns, which had just been published. When he pointed this out to another Lamont researcher, though, the man just laughed and said, "Next thing, you'll be proving [the] Vine and Matthews [theory]."

Pitman knew very little about the Vine-Matthews-Morley hypothesis, but, he told geologist-historian William Glen, "I began

Eltanin 19: "Too Perfect"

In William Glen's *The Road to Jaramillo*, Walter Pitman recalled the following

> I remember staying [at Lamont] all night long one day, running out magnified projected profiles . . . so they look as though you've run perpendicular to a ridge axis. I pinned up all the profiles of Eltanin 19, 20, and 21 on [Neil] Opdyke's door and went home for a bit of rest. When I came back the guy [Opdyke] was just beside himself! He knew that we'd proved seafloor spreading! It was the first time that you could see the total similarity between the profiles. . . . The bilateral symmetry of Eltanin 19 was the absolute crucial thing. Once Opdyke saw that he said, "That's it—you've got it!"

"For a few months Neil's group and ours practically lived in each other's laps," Pitman told another author, William Wertenbaker, as Wertenbaker reports in *The Floor of the Sea*. "His pattern [of normal and reverse magnetizations], that he was getting from sediments, and our pattern were always the same."

to smell something [interesting] at that time." He made a point of reading Vine and Matthews's paper. Then, in January 1966, he went on to analyze the magnetic data from an earlier *Eltanin* cruise, leg 19 (*Eltanin* 19 for short), which had crossed the East Pacific Rise.

Neil Opdyke was keeping a close watch on Pitman's progress. "What he knew, I knew within a day," he said later. Unlike most of the other Lamont researchers, Opdyke believed that the continental drift theory and the related ideas of Hess, Vine, and Matthews were probably right. He hoped that his own research, Pitman's, or both would uncover evidence to support them. When he first saw the magnetic profile from *Eltanin* 19, he could hardly believe his eyes. For about 400 miles (644 km), the symmetry of the pattern on the two sides of the ridge was essentially perfect.

Frederick Vine was even more thrilled than Opdyke. When Vine visited Lamont in February and saw the *Eltanin* 19 profile, he

Nonetheless, persuading James Heirtzler, the head of the paleo-magnetics laboratory, and others at Lamont to share their excitement took hard work. The very fact that the *Eltanin* 19 profile showed a completely symmetrical pattern on both sides of the East Pacific Rise, including all the reversals on the Cox-Doell-Dalrymple time line and many earlier ones besides, made them doubt its reality. The reaction of Lamont scientist Joe Worzel was typical, Pitman told William Glen:

> Worzel looked at [the *Eltanin* 19 profile] for a while and finally said, "Well, that knocks the seafloor-spreading nonsense into a cocked hat." I said, "What do you mean, Joe?" He said, "It's too perfect," and walked out of the room.

In spite of their early skepticism, the naysayers eventually had to admit that the perfection of what came to be called "Pitman's magic profile" actually existed. In April 1966, after Richard Doell, one of the authors of the magnetic reversal timetable, saw the results from Opdyke's cores and the *Eltanin* 19 profile together, he said in a stunned voice, "It's so good it can't possibly be true, but it is."

realized immediately that it proved his hypothesis. "It [is] all over but the shouting," he said. He told Pitman that that was the first time he had been wholly convinced of his own theory.

Pitman (with his supervisor, J. R. Heirtzler) and Frederick Vine both wrote papers about the *Eltanin* 19 profile and its relationship to the Vine-Matthews-Morley theory that were published in the journal *Science* in December 1966. Vine pointed out that he now had three independent confirmations of his idea: his own Juan de Fuca Ridge results, the *Eltanin* 19 profile, and the magnetic profiles from Neil Opdyke's sediment cores.

Shaking Up Geology

Still more confirmation of seafloor spreading soon came from a different geological specialty: seismology. In June 1966, Pitman and Heirtzler showed the *Eltanin*-19 profile to Lynn Sykes (1937–) and Jack Oliver (1923–), two Lamont seismologists. Sykes and Oliver had been studying undersea earthquakes, using a computer program developed at Lamont that could locate the epicenters of such quakes far more accurately than had been possible before. After seeing the "magic" profile, Sykes and Oliver went "roaring back," as Pitman put it to William Wertenbaker, to look at their own data again.

Sykes had been looking for a way to test a theory that John Tuzo Wilson had proposed in a 1965 paper, "A New Class of Faults and Their Bearing on Continental Drift." In this paper, Wilson claimed that the Earth's crust was divided into rigid plates that floated on the asthenosphere. The continents were part of these plates and were carried along with the plates when convection currents in the asthenosphere made the plates move. Plate boundaries, he said, could be of three types: mid-ocean ridges, trenches, or a type of earthquake zone that Wilson called a transform fault. Lamont researchers studying the Mid-Atlantic Ridge had noticed in 1962 that many parts of the ridge were offset, or displaced horizontally with respect to each other, for hundreds of miles, creating a shape that looked more like an uneven staircase than a smooth curve. Wilson placed his transform faults on the offsets, or "steps" of the staircase, which were known to be the sites of frequent earthquakes.

Adjoining plates were pulled apart at the ridges, Wilson said. At the trenches, plates were pushed together, forcing one plate to ride up over the other. Mountains or islands were created on the upper plate, while the edge of the lower plate was pushed down into the trench and absorbed. Transform faults appeared when plates slid past each other, making earthquake zones that ran perpendicular to the line where the plates scraped together. Wilson gave the faults this name because he believed that they were transformed into either a ridge or a trench at their ends, where the earthquake action was known to stop. Ridges, trenches, and

John Tuzo Wilson, a geophysicist at the University of Toronto, is shown here in 1967, about the time that most Earth scientists accepted the theory of plate tectonics. Wilson, in a 1965 article, was the first to describe the Earth's moving crust as being divided into plates. He also showed how the plates interacted with one another and named a new kind of earthquake fault, the transform fault. (University of Toronto Department of Physics)

transform faults were the main spots where the crust was moving, according to Wilson's theory. They were also the places where most volcanoes, earthquakes, and mountains or island arcs appeared.

Sykes had wanted to test Wilson's ideas about transform faults, and his look at the *Eltanin* 19 profile, which seemed to confirm seafloor spreading so strikingly, made him even more determined to do so. Using new, sensitive seismographs that could show the direction of the first motions in quakes, he analyzed earthquakes that had occurred along fracture zones perpendicular to the crests of the Mid-Atlantic Ridge and the East Pacific Rise. "Essentially I knew what I had inside a week," he told William Wertenbaker. "I looked at twenty earthquakes and they all worked." Sykes had expected to disprove Wilson's theory, but the motions he found in fact fitted with what Wilson had predicted. "They were exactly the opposite of what classical geology predicts for horizontal fault motion," Sykes said. "Sea floor spreading was the only thing that could produce those earthquakes."

Sykes, Oliver, and another Lamont seismologist Bryan Isacks (1936–   ), also had been trying to confirm another part of the sea-floor spreading theory by studying deep earthquakes—those centered in the mantle rather than the crust. Such earthquakes had been found to occur only under trenches and island arcs, the very spots (called subduction zones) where Hess had suggested that his "jaw crusher" was pulling pieces of crust down into the mantle. In late 1966, the group concluded from their earthquake data that a 60-mile (97-km) thick slab of crust was being dragged down near Tonga, a group of islands in the South Pacific. "All of a sudden, it became very simple and obvious," Sykes told William Wertenbaker. "We were led to the conclusion that the [deep] earthquake zone is the same as the seafloor, and then . . . that the seafloor was being pushed, or pulled, down into the mantle to form the zone." The motion was causing the earthquakes. Subduction provided the other half of the process begun by seafloor spreading, recycling the crust and keeping the overall amount of crust the same.

Mathematical Support

Wilson's 1965 paper had been the first to present a complete theory that tied seafloor spreading to continental drift. In 1967, Jason Morgan (1935–   ) provided mathematical support for Wilson's ideas about plate movement. Morgan, like Hess and Vine, was a member of the Princeton University geology department. With the help of a computer and a mathematical formula called Euler's theorem, Morgan calculated how rigid blocks—an approximation of Wilson's plates—would move on the surface of a sphere. He used the three types of boundaries (ridges, trenches, and transform faults) that Wilson had discussed. The results fitted extremely well with the actual movements that had been observed. A Cambridge University geophysicist Dan McKenzie (1942–   ) did much the same thing at about the same time.

Xavier Le Pichon (1937–   ), a French scientist visiting Lamont, applied Morgan's method to what was known about the magnetic anomalies, the seismic data, and reconstruction of past plate motions. Like Morgan, Le Pichon found that mathematically modeling the rotation of rigid plates around an axis could account for the different amounts, as well as kinds, of geological activity at the undersea ridges, the trenches, and the fracture zones or transform faults, as well as in the interior of the plates. "All movements [of plates] are interconnected," Le Pichon emphasized when he presented his work at the 1967 meeting of the American Geophysical Union. "Any major changes in the pattern of spreading must be global."

Jason Morgan of Princeton University created a mathematical model showing how rigid blocks might move on a sphere. Morgan's work provided a mathematical underpinning for the theory of plate tectonics. (Trustees of Princeton University)

A New Theory of Earth Movement

All these ideas and pieces of research came together in three key geological meetings in 1966 and 1967. The American Geophysical Union held two of these meetings in April 1966 and April 1967 in Washington, D.C. The third meeting took place in November 1966 at the Goddard Institute for Space Studies in New York and was sponsored by the National Aeronautics and Space Administration (NASA).

These meetings were as important to the acceptance of the new theory of the Earth as the New York oil geology meeting 40 years before had been to the rejection of Alfred Wegener's ideas. They ended what William Wertenbaker in his 1974 book, *The Floor of the Sea,* calls a "period of almost unbearable excitement" that some have termed "the most remarkable period in the history of geology." By the end of 1967, the opinion of almost every member of the geological community about the idea that the continents could move had reversed as abruptly as the planet's magnetic poles sometimes had done.

Bryan Isacks, Lynn Sykes, and Jack Oliver pulled all the research together in a paper titled "Seismology and the New Global Tectonics," which was published in the *Journal of Geophysical Research* in September 1968. Expanding on the ideas of Hess, Vine, Wilson, and others, this paper outlined a new overarching theory of the Earth's movement called plate tectonics, after a Greek word meaning "to build." It held that the Earth's crust and uppermost mantle, down to about 62 miles (100 km), is rigid and has significant resistance to earthquake waves. This combined zone, the lithosphere, overlies the asthenosphere, a zone of hot rock that extends down to about 435 miles (700 km). The asthenosphere is solid, but in the long course of geologic time it can flow like a thick liquid.

The lithosphere is divided into seven large and about a dozen smaller plates. Islands and continents are the parts of the plates that show above sea level. Impelled by forces in the asthenosphere that are still poorly understood, the plates move slowly around the globe. Crust is created at some spots on the seafloor and destroyed in equal amounts at others, keeping the planet the same size.

From the first days of its acceptance to the present, writers have given high praise to the plate tectonics theory. In *A Revolution in the Earth Sciences,* published in 1973, science historian Anthony Hallam called plate tectonics "the biggest advance in Earth science since acceptance in the early nineteenth century of the paradigms of uniformitarianism and stratigraphical correlation of fossils [the idea that fossils could be used to show the age of rock layers] established geology as a true science."

The acceptance of plate tectonics brought profound changes, not only to Earth scientists' understanding of the history of Earth's crust, but to their view of the planet as a whole—and of the scientific disciplines that study it. As John Tuzo Wilson said in 1968, plate tectonics showed that "the Earth, instead of appearing as an inert statue, is a living, mobile thing." The theory emphasized how much Earth had changed in the past and is still changing. At the same time, it demonstrated that some supposed changes that

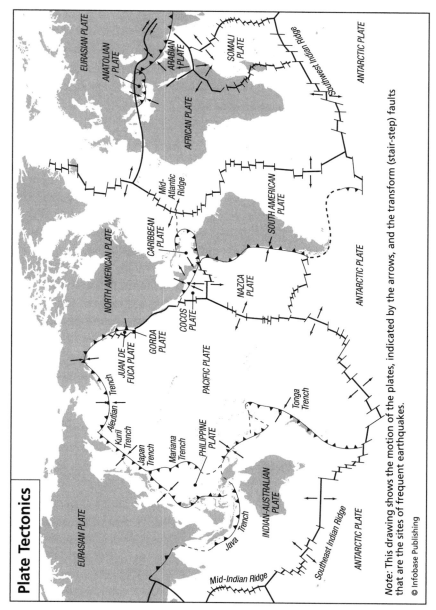

Plate Tectonics

Note: This drawing shows the motion of the plates, indicated by the arrows, and the transform (stair-step) faults that are the sites of frequent earthquakes.

© Infobase Publishing

The theory of plate tectonics, descended from Alfred Wegener's continental drift theory, became widely accepted in the mid-1960s. It states that the Earth's crust is divided into seven large and about a dozen smaller plates. These plates are constantly in motion, pushed by convection currents and other forces in the mantle below. Earthquakes and volcanic eruptions occur in places where plates collide or rub against one another.

geologists had long accepted were false: the planet was neither shrinking nor expanding.

"The new view of the Earth [plate tectonics] was revolutionary . . . because it was a global theory in the dual sense of being a whole-Earth theory and a theory which drew upon and drew together all fields of the [Earth] science," H. E. LeGrand wrote in *Drifting Continents and Shifting Theories.* Rather than describing particular areas or rock formations, plate tectonics encompassed the entire planet, which it portrayed as a system of interacting parts. The theory helped scientists realize that—just as Alfred Wegener had urged—such a system could be understood only when researchers from many fields worked together. It is probably no accident that scientists began using the umbrella term "Earth science" at about the same time that they accepted the new worldview of plate tectonics.

Finally, plate tectonics marked a turn away from the strictly descriptive fieldwork so popular in Wegener's day toward the kind of overarching theory that Wegener had proposed. John Tuzo Wilson emphasized and praised this change. Instead of simply describing changes that had occurred in the past, Wilson said, Earth science could now focus on explaining those past changes and predicting future ones.

> *The acceptance of continental drift [in the new form of plate tectonics] has transformed the Earth sciences from a group of rather unimaginative studies based upon pedestrian interpretations of natural phenomena into a unified science that holds the promise of great intellectual and practical advances.*

Why did the community of Earth scientists accept plate tectonics so quickly when it had resisted continental drift for so long? No doubt there were several reasons. Science historian Naomi Oreskes thinks that one reason was that so much of the evidence supporting plate tectonics came from geophysics. Geophysics depends on direct measurements and mathematical calculations, so it is difficult to dispute. By contrast, most of Alfred Wegener's evidence for continental drift came from supposed similarities between rock formations or fossils in different parts of the world. It is easy to disagree about how similar two things really are, and similarities often can be explained in more than one way.

Another reason may have been that in the case of plate tectonics, the Earth science community itself decided that the evidence was convincing enough to make the theory acceptable. Wegener assembled research findings from many scientists and stated that they provided clear proof of his idea, but his critics accused him of selecting only the studies that agreed with him. For plate tectonics, the scientists made their own selections and judgments.

Finally, according to Anthony Hallam, plate tectonics succeeded because it met the requirements for a useful theory. "By the criteria normally used to judge the quality of scientific theories, namely precision, scope, explanatory value, and testability, plate tectonics scores highly," Hallam wrote in *A Revolution in the Earth Sciences*. In the late 1960s and 1970s, researchers applied the new theory to many areas of Earth science and solved longstanding puzzles, such as the way mountains are formed.

Plate Tectonics Today

Earth scientists still feel that the theory of plate tectonics is the best description of the way the Earth's crust is formed and destroyed and interacts. New techniques and tools have led to new discoveries about plate movement, however, and the theory has been modified to reflect these new findings.

Researchers concluded by the 1970s, for instance, that some parts of Harry Hess's theory of seafloor spreading, which underlay plate tectonics, were oversimplified. New research suggested that convection currents alone may not be strong enough to move the crustal plates. Some Earth scientists think that gravity may be the chief moving force, dragging cold, dense pieces of crust down into the mantle at subduction zones and pulling the attached plates along with them. Others believe that large-scale currents in the mantle do account for most of the motion, but the currents are more complex than those that Hess described.

Also in the 1970s, Earth scientists learned that plates often carry with them small pieces of other plates, called terranes. Terranes scrape off one plate and stick to another during collisions between plates, much as paint might rub off on a person's jacket when the person brushes against a newly painted fence. Terranes are most often transferred when one plate is pulled under another. The border between the terrane and the plate it lies upon is often marked by an earthquake fault. Terranes also can be identified because their characteristics are different from those of the rocks around them. Some areas, such as parts of North America's western coast, are complex patchworks of terranes from different sources.

Classic plate tectonics proposed that plates move at a steady rate overall, but that may not always have been true. Paul Silver of the Carnegie Institution of Washington and Mark Behn of the Wood Hole Oceanographic Institution said in 2008 that they had found evidence that about a billion years ago, plate motion—specifically, subduction—stopped almost entirely for a while. Their conclusion was based on measurements of the rate at which the Earth gives off heat. If the planet had always released heat at its present rate, the researchers said, it should be cooler than it is. A periodic slowdown or stopping of plate movement could explain how the heat was retained. "If the tectonic plates are moving, the Earth releases more heat and cools down faster," Behn said. "If you don't have those cracked and moving plates, then heat has to get out by diffusing through the solid rock, which is much slower." According to *Space Daily*, which reported the research, Silver and Behn concluded that "rather than being continuous, plate tectonics may work intermittently through Earth history, turning on and off as the planet remakes itself."

The way in which pieces of crust sink into the mantle also may differ from the original plate tectonics picture. A team of British and Swiss scientists reported in early 2008 that, contrary to what experts had thought, the edges of old, heavy plates may be dragged only as far as the boundary between the upper and the lower mantle. They then flatten out and lie on top of the boundary. This is happening near Tonga, the Mariana Islands, and Japan. Younger, more flexible plates, on the other hand, bend and fold at the boundary for tens of millions of years, then reach a critical mass and sink rapidly into the lower mantle, dragging the rest of the plate after them at high speed.

The scientists believe that this is occurring in Central and South America, where movements have been more rapid than researchers would expect for such young plates.

Some new information about plate tectonics comes from new technology, such as satellites. Scientists began using satellites to track plate motion in the 1980s. They have determined that the continents move an average of 1.6 inches (4 cm) each year. Satellites with radar altimeters map the ocean floor by recording bulges and dips on the ocean's surface that reflect the topography far below. Other satellites detect gravity anomalies like the ones that intrigued George Everest and Felix Vening Meinesz.

In 2006, images from the European Space Agency's Envisat satellite showed a new piece of crust being created—not at sea but on (or rather below) land. Tim Wright of the University of Leeds, leader of an international team that interpreted the satellite results, reported that a huge rift, 37 miles (60 km) long and up to 26 feet (8 m) wide, was opening beneath the dry, barren Afar region of Ethiopia. This area, long known for its volcanic eruptions and earthquakes, lies at the border between the Arabian and Nubian tectonic plates. The crust is stretched thin there, and an upsurge of molten magma tore it open. The rift was the largest ever spotted by satellite monitoring. "The process happening here is identical to that which created the Atlantic Ocean," Wright told the *Guardian*. "If this continues, we believe parts of Eritrea, Ethiopia and Djibouti will sink low enough to allow water to flow in from the Red Sea."

Some researchers have focused on the past and the future of plate tectonics. Hubert Staudigel of the Scripps Institution of Oceanography reported in 2007 that ancient rocks from southern Greenland—the oldest known pieces of Earth's crust—indicated that the continents were moving 3.8 billion years ago, very early in the planet's 4.5-billion-year history. Looking at the other end of the tectonic time cycle, Christopher Scotese, a geologist at the University of Texas at Arlington, believes that 250 million years from now, the continents will converge once more into a new Pangaea, which he calls Pangaea Ultima.

Earth scientists will continue to investigate the way the planet's crust moves and has moved in the past. Perhaps their discoveries will merely refine the understanding of the planet that plate tectonics provides, as has happened so far. It is equally possible, though, that they will uncover something completely new. Their findings may alter scientific opinion as radically as the discoveries in paleomagnetism, seismology, and other fields altered the Earth science community's view of continental drift in the 1960s. Such a surprise can always happen, because science—like the Earth itself—never stops changing.

Conclusion:
Reaching into the Future

Alfred Wegener's continental drift is not the same as the theory of plate tectonics. Wegener presented a completely different picture of how and why the continents move than plate tectonics does. Nonetheless, just as creatures as diverse as mice, elephants, and human beings evolved from the simple mammals that hid in the forests where dinosaurs roamed, so plate tectonics evolved from continental drift. The two theories share the basic idea that the Earth's crust, both land and sea, is undergoing slow but constant change. As part of that change, even the largest landmasses and the widest oceans may alter their positions on the globe.

Wegener gathered from a wide range of geological fields what he felt was an impressive quantity of evidence to support his theory—but it was not enough. His critics were quick to point out that some of his information was inaccurate and some could be, or even had to be, interpreted in ways other than the ones he suggested. He (and the scientists who ridiculed him) lacked the data that would later provide such convincing support for plate tectonics. Some of that data came from fields such as paleomagnetism, which did not even exist in Wegener's time.

What Wegener did have was what F. K. Mather, editor of an influential reference book called *The Source Book of Geology,* called "one of the most fertile geological imaginations of this century." That imagination let him build the seemingly trivial observation of similarities in the outlines of Africa and South America into a complete picture of the Earth's dynamic past.

Underlying and guiding that imagination, according to people who knew him, was a powerful instinct for recognizing which items in the welter of facts and ideas that make up any science were truly important. "Wegener possessed a sense for the significant that seldom erred," Hans Benndorf, a colleague, wrote in a memorial essay. W. Wundt, another acquaintance, elaborated on the same idea:

> *Alfred Wegener . . . had an extraordinary talent for observation and knowing what is . . . both simple and important, and what can be expected to give a result. Added to this was a rigorous logic, which enabled him to assemble rightly everything relevant to his ideas.*

Wegener also had the courage to believe in his imagination. He refused to abandon his plans and goals, no matter what challenges he faced. He showed this determination most obviously in his career as an Arctic explorer. "He was a man of action, whose iron will and unflagging energy led him to extraordinary achievements," Hans Benndorf wrote. His courage was not limited to physical challenges. He revealed it just as clearly in the persistence with which he advocated his drift theory in the face of powerful opposition. Each new edition of his book included answers to his critics and additional evidence to support his ideas.

Because of these qualities, Alfred Wegener was able to do something that few people, in science or any other form of human activity, can achieve: He stepped beyond his own time. His ideas were too strange for most of his contemporaries to appreciate, but they survived to inspire a later generation of scientists who had not even been born at the time he lost his life on the unforgiving Arctic ice. Those scientists, in turn, applied new knowledge and technologies and succeeded where Wegener, through little fault of his own, had failed. They persuaded the Earth science community that the once-despised theory of moving continents was right and, in doing so, created a new vision of a dynamic, ever-changing Earth. "As the man who really started it all," Anthony Hallam wrote in *A Revolution in the Earth Sciences*, "Alfred Wegener deserves wider recognition as one of the most important scientific innovators of . . . [the 20th] century."

CHRONOLOGY

1644   René Descartes offers the first complete scientific theory of Earth's origin, history, and structure.

1830   Charles Lyell publishes the first edition of *Principles of Geology*, which establishes the principle of uniformitarianism.

1840   George Everest discovers gravity abnormalities in the Himalayas, leading to development of the theory of isostasy.

November 1, 1880   Alfred Wegener is born in Berlin.

1903–04   Scientists discover that radioactive elements give off heat when they decay and are common in rocks, providing a new way of determining the age of rocks and a new heat source for the earth.

November 24, 1904   Wegener earns a Ph.D. in astronomy from Friedrich Wilhelm University.

1905   Wegener begins working at the Royal Prussian Aeronautical Observatory in Lindenberg.

1907–08   Wegener is the meteorologist on the *Danmark* expedition to Greenland.

1909   Wegener becomes a *Privatdozent* at Marburg University.

1910	Frank Bursley Taylor publishes a theory of continental drift.
Christmas 1910	Wegener notices that the outlines of Africa and South America in a friend's atlas appear to fit together.
1911	Wegener publishes textbook *Thermodynamics of the Atmosphere.*
Fall 1911	Wegener sees a book showing similarity of fossil animals in West Africa and Brazil; he begins seeking evidence that Africa and South America might once have been joined.
January 1912	Wegener gives talks on his continental drift theory in two scientific meetings.
1912–13	Wegener goes on a second expedition to Greenland with Johan Peter Koch and two others.
1913	Wegener marries Else Köppen.
1914	Wegener serves in Belgium during World War I and is injured twice.
1915	Wegener publishes the first edition of *The Origin of Continents and Oceans.*
1918	World War I ends with Germany's defeat; Wegener returns to Marburg.
1919	Wegener succeeds Wladimir Köppen as director of the theoretical meteorology department at the German Marine Observatory and moves to Hamburg.

1920	Wegener publishes the second edition of *The Origin of Continents and Oceans.*
1922	Wegener publishes the third edition of *The Origin of Continents and Oceans*; the first reviews of his work in English appear.
1923	South African geologist Alexander du Toit finds close similarity between rock formations in South Africa and parts of South America.
1924	Wegener and Wladimir Köppen coauthor *The Climates of the Geological Past*; *The Origin of Continents and Oceans* is translated into English for the first time; Wegener becomes professor of meteorology and geophysics at the University of Graz.
November 15, 1926	The American Association of Petroleum Geologists holds a conference on continental drift in New York, during which most speakers strongly criticize Wegener's theory.
1929	Wegener publishes the fourth edition of *The Origin of Continents and Oceans.*
March–November 1929	Wegener, Johannes Georgi, and two others go to Greenland to make preparations for a major expedition.
1930	In "Radioactivity and Earth Movements," Arthur Holmes explains how convection currents in a lower layer of the Earth might make the planet's crust move.
April 1, 1930	Wegener's final expedition to Greenland begins.
June 17, 1930	After a delay of more than a month due to frozen sea ice, Wegener's group begins setting up their West Station.

July 30, 1930 Johannes Georgi begins setting up the Mid-Ice station.

October 30, 1930 Wegener, Fritz Loewe, and Rasmus Villumsen reach Mid-Ice on a final supply trip.

November 1, 1930 Wegener and Villumsen leave Mid-Ice, planning to return to West Station.

November 2, 1930 Wegener dies, probably from a heart attack; Villumsen buries him in the ice and attempts to continue the journey.

May 8, 1931 A relief party from West Station finds Wegener's body.

mid-August, 1931 The Greenland expedition ends.

1930s Felix Vening Meinesz's measurements of gravity in the deep sea support the idea that convection currents in a lower layer are moving parts of the Earth's crust; using undersea seismology, Maurice Ewing shows that the crust of the seafloor is much thinner and younger than had been thought.

1932 Bailey Willis suggests that continents were once joined by "isthmian links," an alternative to the continental drift theory.

1937 Alexander du Toit describes his version of continental drift in *Our Wandering Continents.*

1940s, 1950s World War II and the cold war spur military interest in the deep sea and an explosion of marine science research.

1944 Arthur Holmes expands on his convection current theory in an influential textbook, *Principles of Physical Geology.*

1952   Marie Tharp suggests that the Mid-Atlantic
                        Ridge is divided by a rift valley, possibly a
                        place where the crust was dividing and new
                        crust was being created.

1955   Stanley Runcorn finds paleomagnetic evi-
                        dence that the magnetic poles, the conti-
                        nents, or both have moved in the past.

1955–56   Scripps scientists Ronald Mason and Arthur
                        Raff find a striped magnetic pattern in sea-
                        floor rocks around an undersea ridge.

1956–57   Bruce Heezen and Maurice Ewing describe
                        the mid-ocean ridge system, attracting new
                        attention to the possibility of continental drift.

1962   Harry Hess publishes his theory of seafloor
                        spreading.

September 1963   Frederick Vine and Drummond Matthews
                        propose a theory connecting magnetic
                        striping to seafloor spreading.

1965   Vine and John Tuzo Wilson publish mag-
                        netic striping patterns around the Juan de
                        Fuca Ridge and show that they are similar
                        to patterns predicted by a computer model
                        of seafloor spreading; Wilson publishes a
                        second paper describing how plates in the
                        Earth's crust interact and naming a new type
                        of earthquake fault.

late 1965   Neil Opdyke analyzes magnetic patterns in
                        sediment cores; Walter Pitman begins analyz-
                        ing magnetic profiles obtained by the *Eltanin*.

January 1966   Pitman finds a section of a profile from
                        Eltanin 19 that shows perfect symmetry on
                        both sides of an undersea ridge.

February 1966 — Vine sees the *Eltanin* 19 profile and realizes that it offers a major proof of his theory.

late 1966 — Lynn Sykes and his coworkers confirm Wilson's theory of transform faults; they also find evidence that a slab of crust is being pulled into the mantle near Tonga.

April 1966, November 1966, April 1967 — Three key scientific meetings bring together the lines of research that support the new theory of plate tectonics and convince most Earth scientists to accept the theory.

1967 — Jason Morgan provides a mathematical model for the movements of crustal plates on the Earth's surface.

September 1968 — Bryan Isacks, Lynn Sykes, and Jack Oliver publish a paper describing the theory of plate tectonics.

1970s — Researchers conclude that parts of Hess's seafloor spreading theory are too simple; they discover that plates may sometimes pick up small pieces of other plates (terranes) during collisions.

1980 — The Alfred Wegener Institute is founded in Bremerhaven, Germany.

1980s — Earth scientists begin to use satellites to study plate tectonics.

2006 — Satellite images show new crust being created under Ethiopia.

2007 — Ancient rocks from Greenland indicate that plates were moving 3.8 billion years ago.

2008   Researchers say that plate movement may have changed its rate of speed or even stopped at times in the past; they revise ideas about the way crust moves down into the mantle.

GLOSSARY

asthenosphere the layer of Earth's mantle that lies just below the lithosphere, extending from about 62 miles (100 km) to 435 miles (700 km) below the planet's surface; it is solid but soft and can flow like a thick liquid over geologic time

basalt a dark, fine-grained rock, formed from cooling lava; it is believed to make up the bulk of the seafloor surface, as well as being deposited on land by volcanic eruptions

catastrophism the belief that Earth's past history was marked by events more violent than any that can be observed today

continental drift Alfred Wegener's theory that the continents can move horizontally on the Earth's surface and had different arrangements in early geologic times than they do now

convection cell a more or less rectangular pattern of upward-moving and downward-moving convection currents

convection currents currents that cause movement in a liquid when different parts of the liquid are at different temperatures; heated parts of the liquid expand and rise, cooler parts shrink and fall

Curie point a temperature point, named after French chemist Pierre Curie, at which an iron-containing rock becomes magnetized, taking on the direction and polarity of the Earth's magnetic field, if the rock is being cooled; if the rock is being heated, it loses its existing magnetic alignment when it passes this temperature

deductive reasoning reasoning from the general to the particular; for instance, using a theory or hypothesis to make a prediction about what will happen under particular conditions

density mass per unit of volume

echo sounder a device that identifies objects or surface topography by sending out sound waves and recording the echoes that bounce off the object or surface

eon the largest division in the geological timescale; eons, such as the Proterozoic, are divided into eras

epoch   the largest division in the paleomagnetic timescale; the scale has four epochs, named after magnetism pioneers Brunhes, Matuyama, Gauss, and Gilbert

era   the second-largest division in the geological timescale; eras, such as the Paleozoic, are divided into periods

event   a smaller division in the paleomagnetic timescale, representing a relatively brief change in the Earth's magnetic field; events are named after places, such as Jaramillo (in New Mexico)

geodesy   the Earth science field that measures the size and shape of the Earth

geology   the Earth science that studies the origin, history, and structure of the Earth, especially as reflected in the rocks of the planet's crust

geophysics   the Earth science that studies the physical properties of the Earth

Gondwanaland (or Gondwana)   the name given by Alfred Wegener and others to a southern supercontinent thought to have existed until about 145 million years ago; it included what are now Africa, South America, India, Australia, and Antarctica

granite   a common kind of light-colored igneous rock, less dense and heavy than basalt; rocks related to granite are thought to make up most of Earth's landmasses

gravimeter   a device that measures minute local variations in the Earth's gravity field

guyot   a type of flat-topped undersea volcano first identified by Harry Hess; Hess believed that the tops of the guyots were originally above water and were worn down by erosion, after which the mountains slowly sank as a consequence of crustal movement caused by sea-floor spreading

hypothesis   a tentative general statement about the cause or workings of natural phenomena

igneous rock   a rock formed from molten materials that have cooled and hardened

inductive reasoning   reasoning from the particular to the general; for instance, combining information from a number of observations or experiments to create a general statement (hypothesis or theory)

isostasy   the balance between gravity and buoyancy that adjusts the height and depth of objects floating in a liquid, particularly portions of the Earth's solid crust floating in the liquidlike sima or asthenosphere

lithosphere   the Earth's crust and upper mantle, extending to about 62 miles (100 km) below the surface; it is divided into plates and floats on the softer asthenosphere

magma   molten rock beneath the Earth's surface

magnetometer   a device that can measure local variations in the Earth's magnetic field

mantle   the layer of the Earth located below the crust, extending between about 20 miles (33 km) and 1,802 miles (2,900 km) below the surface

meteorology   the Earth science that studies the Earth's atmosphere and weather

mid-ocean ridge system   a system consisting of parallel ranges of undersea mountains, with a narrow rift valley between them, that curves through the center of the world's oceans like the seam on a baseball; seafloor spreading and creation of new crust occurs in the rift valleys

Mohorovicic discontinuity (Moho)   the depth (about 5 miles [8 km] below the ocean floors and an average of 20 miles [32 km] beneath the continents) at which earthquake waves change velocity abruptly, marking the boundary between the Earth's crust and the mantle; it is named after Croatian seismologist Andrija Mohorovičić

neptunist theory   a theory espoused by German geologist Abraham Gottlob Werner and his followers in the late 18th and early 19th centuries, which stated that most of Earth's surface features had been shaped chiefly by currents in the ocean that originally covered the planet

paleoclimatology   the Earth science field that studies Earth's climates in the geological past

paleontology   the Earth science that studies the remains of ancient living things preserved in rocks (fossils)

Pangaea   the name that Alfred Wegener gave to the protocontinent that, he said, contained all of Earth's landmasses until about 250 million years ago

period   the third-largest unit in the geologic timescale; eras are divided into periods, such as the Jurassic, and periods in turn are divided into epochs

permanentism   the belief, held by many American geologists in the late 19th century, that the Earth's continents and oceans have always occupied approximately the same locations that they have now

plate   one of a number of solid blocks into which the Earth's crust is divided, according to the theory of plate tectonics; the crust is thought to consist of seven large and about a dozen smaller plates

plate tectonics   a theory describing the creation, destruction, and movements of the Earth's crust that was proposed in 1967 and quickly accepted by the Earth science community; it is descended from Alfred Wegener's continental drift theory

plutonist theory   a theory espoused by James Hutton and his followers in the early 19th century, which stated that Earth's surface features had been shaped chiefly by the planet's internal heat

Pohlflucht   a small force (literally, pole-fleeing force), created by centrifugal force from the Earth's rotation and by the bulge at the slightly flattened Earth's equator, whose increased gravity pulled landmasses toward it; Alfred Wegener thought that *Pohlflucht* was one of the forces that made continents move horizontally

polarity   the alignment of a magnet (or iron crystals in magnetic material) toward either the north or the south magnetic pole of the Earth; the polarity of the Earth's magnetic field has reversed many times in the geologic past

polar wandering   the idea that the Earth's poles (geological, magnetic, or both) had different locations during the geological past than they have now

progressivism   the belief that the forces affecting the Earth's crust in the geologic past are the same as the forces affecting it now, but those forces may have acted at different intensities or rates of speed in the past

radioactive decay   the breakdown of radioactive forms (isotopes) of certain elements into nonradioactive elements; this process takes place at a fixed rate and can therefore be used to determine the age of materials containing the isotopes

seafloor spreading   a theory proposed by Harry Hess in 1960 that states that new crust is created when molten rock pushes up through the seafloor at mid-ocean ridges and destroyed when slabs of crust are pulled down into the mantle at undersea trenches; this process, driven by convection currents in the mantle, moves the crust of the Earth, including the continents, as if they were on a conveyor belt

sedimentary rock   rock formed by the solidification of particles that sink to the bottom of oceans

seismograph   a device that measures vibrations produced by earthquakes or by artificial earthquakes deliberately created by explosions

seismology the Earth science that studies earthquakes and other vibrations that move through the layers of the Earth, whether natural or produced by humans

sial Alfred Wegener's term for the uppermost layer of the Earth's crust, made of granite and similar rocks; sial made up the planet's landmasses but formed only a thin layer on the seafloor

sima Alfred Wegener's term for the layer of crust that lay beneath the sial; he thought that the sima, though solid, could flow like a liquid over long periods of time, allowing the continents to move through it

subduction zone a spot where part of a crustal plate is being pulled down into the mantle at an oceanic trench

terrane a small piece of a crustal plate that is scraped off onto another plate when the two plates collide; the terrane becomes attached to the second plate and is carried away with it

theory a general description of the cause or behavior of a group of phenomena in nature that has been well tested and is usually accepted as true

thermodynamics the study of heat in relationship to other forms of energy

transform fault a type of earthquake fault, first described by John Tuzo Wilson in 1965, that forms when crustal plates slide past each other; the fault runs perpendicular to the line where the plates scrape together and is transformed into a ridge or a trench at its ends

uniformitarianism the doctrine, established by Charles Lyell in the early 19th century, that all forces that affected the Earth in the past can still be seen in action today; this doctrine is sometimes held to include the idea that those forces always acted at the same intensity and rate of speed that they have today

Vine-Matthews-Morley hypothesis the idea, first proposed in 1963, that the striped patterns of normal and reverse magnetism seen in rocks around mid-ocean ridges were associated with seafloor spreading; it predicted that the magnetic patterns on the two sides of a ridge should be mirror images of one another

viscous thick, or resistant to flow (a property of a liquid or a liquidlike material)

FURTHER RESOURCES

Books

"Alfred Wegener." In *Scientists: Their Lives and Works,* Vols. 1–7. Farmington Hills, Mich.: Gale Group, 2006. Available online through Biography Resource Center. Accessed December 8, 2007.

> *Brief biography of Wegener, including a description of his continental drift theory.*

du Toit, Alexander. *A Geological Comparison of South America with South Africa.* Washington, D.C.: Carnegie Institution of Washington, 1927.

> *Du Toit, an expert in the geology of his native South Africa, notes many similarities between South African rock formations and those he observed in parts of South America.*

———. *Our Wandering Continents: An Hypothesis of Continental Drifting.* London: Oliver & Boyd, 1937.

> *In this book, du Toit describes his modified version of Alfred Wegener's continental drift theory.*

Glen, William. *The Road to Jaramillo: Critical Years of the Revolution in Earth Science.* Stanford, Calif.: Stanford University Press, 1991.

> *A description of the exciting decade of research (1957–66) that led to the acceptance of plate tectonics, featuring interviews with the scientists who carried it out.*

Hallam, A. *Great Geological Controversies,* 2nd ed. New York: Oxford University Press, 1989.

> *Includes chapters on neptunism and plutonism, catastrophism and uniformitarianism, the age of the Earth, and continental drift.*

———. *A Revolution in the Earth Sciences: From Continental Drift to Plate Tectonics.* New York: Oxford University Press, 1973.

Describes Alfred Wegener's theory of continental drift, contemporary reactions to it, and how it evolved into the theory of plate tectonics, which became widely accepted in the mid-1960s.

Hess, Harry Hammond. "History of the Ocean Basins." In *Petrologic Studies: A Volume to Honor A. F. Buddington,* edited by A. E. J. Engel, H. L. James, and B. F. Leonard, pp. 599–620. New York: Geological Society of America, 1962.

Hess's scientific description of his theory of seafloor spreading, which he called "an essay in geopoetry."

Holmes, Arthur. *Principles of Physical Geology.* New York: Ronald Press, 1946.

Influential textbook that includes Holmes's version of the continental drift theory, in which he proposes that parts of the crust are moved on Earth's surface by convection currents in the soft layer underlying the crust.

Lawrence, David M. *Upheaval from the Abyss: Ocean Floor Mapping and the Earth Science Revolution.* New Brunswick, N.J.: Rutgers University Press, 2002.

Shows how new discoveries about the ocean floor in the 1950s and 1960s transformed Alfred Wegener's rejected ideas on continental drift into the accepted theory of plate tectonics.

LeGrand, H. E. *Drifting Continents and Shifting Theories.* New York: Cambridge University Press, 1988.

Focuses on other scientists' reactions to the idea of continental drift and discusses why scientists rejected the theory when Alfred Wegener proposed it, yet accepted a revised version of it several decades later.

Lyell, Charles. *Principles of Geology.* New York: Penguin Classics, 1998.

Reissue of the book that established the fundamental geological principle of uniformitarianism.

Marvin, Ursula B. *Continental Drift: The Evolution of a Concept.* Washington, D.C.: Smithsonian Institution Press, 1973.

Provides an account of the geological discoveries and beliefs against which Wegener's continental drift theory was set, as well as explaining the theory, reactions to it, and the research that changed Earth scientists' opinions of it.

McCoy, Roger M. *Ending in Ice: The Revolutionary Idea and Tragic Expedition of Alfred Wegener.* New York: Oxford University Press, 2006.

A biography of Wegener that focuses on his Greenland expeditions, especially the 1930–31 expedition in which he lost his life.

Oreskes, Naomi, ed. *Plate Tectonics: An Insider's History of the Modern Theory of the Earth.* Boulder, Colo.: Westview Press, 2001.

Anthology of articles written by the scientists who took part in the research that established plate tectonics, describing their work and feelings.

———. *The Rejection of Continental Drift: Theory and Method in American Earth Science.* New York: Oxford University Press, 1999.

Concentrates on beliefs about geology and ways of doing science held by geologists of Wegener's time and later; discusses how these attitudes influenced reactions to his theory.

Runcorn, Stanley, K., ed. *Continental Drift.* New York: Academic Press, 1962.

Anthology of scientific papers in which Runcorn and other scientists present new evidence that might lead Earth scientists to reconsider continental drift.

Schwarzbach, Martin, translated by Carla Love. *Alfred Wegener: The Father of Continental Drift.* Madison, Wisc.: Science Tech, 1986.

Full-length biography of Alfred Wegener; includes a memoir by Johannes Georgi and a description of the evolution of continental drift into plate tectonics by I. Bernard Cohen.

Van der Gracht, W., et al. *Theory of Continental Drift: A Symposium on the Origin and Movement of Land Masses . . . as Proposed by Alfred Wegener.* Tulsa, Okla.: American Association of Petroleum Geologists, 1928.

Collection of papers from an influential 1926 symposium in which most of the speakers criticized Wegener's theory, effectively ending most scientists' interest in it for more than three decades.

Wegener, Alfred, translated by John Biram. *The Origin of Continents and Oceans.* Mineola, N.Y.: Dover Publications, 1966.

New English translation of the fourth (1929) edition of Wegener's book, which describes his theory of continental drift and provides supporting evidence from a variety of geological specialties.

Wertenbaker, William. *The Floor of the Sea: Maurice Ewing and the Search to Understand the Earth.* Boston: Little, Brown, 1974.

Focuses on the role of Maurice Ewing and the Lamont Geological Observatory in the deep-sea research that led to the establishment of plate tectonics.

Yount, Lisa. *Modern Marine Science: Exploring the Deep.* New York: Chelsea House, 2006.

For young adults. Includes a chapter on Bruce Heezen, Marie Tharp, and the discovery of the mid-ocean ridge system and another chapter on Harry Hess, seafloor spreading, and the development of plate tectonics.

Internet Resources

Aber, James S. "Alfred Wegener." Emporia State University, *History of Geology.* Available online. URL: http://academic.emporia.edu/aberjame/histgeol/wegener/wegener.htm. Accessed December 8, 2007.

Brief biography of Wegener includes contemporary reactions to his work and a historical assessment.

"The Alfred Wegener Institute." Alfred Wegener Institute. Last updated April 25, 2005. Available online. URL: http://www.awi-bremerhaven.de/AWI. Accessed December 8, 2007.

Brief description of a German institute for polar and marine research established in 1980 in honor of Alfred Wegener.

"A Brief Introduction to Plate Tectonics, Based on the Work of Alfred Wegener." Eastern Illinois University. Available online. URL: http://www.ux1.eiu.edu/~cfjps/1300/cont_drift.html. Accessed June 3, 2008.

Describes and illustrates the evidence that Alfred Wegener offered in 1915 to support his theory of continental drift.

Egger, Anne E. "Plate Tectonics I: The Evidence for a Geologic Revolution." Visionlearning, 2003. Available online. URL: http://www.visionlearning.com/library/module_viewer.php?mid=65. Accessed May 4, 2008.

Focuses on the theories that led up to plate tectonics, especially those of Alfred Wegener, Harry Hess, and Frederick Vine and Drummond Matthews.

———. "Plate Tectonics II: Plates, Plate Boundaries, and Driving Forces." Visionlearning, 2003. Available online. URL: http://www.visionlearning.com/library/module_viewer.php?mid=66. Accessed May 4, 2008.

Describes the plate tectonics theory, focusing on plate boundaries and the different ways that plates can interact with one another.

"The History of Continental Drift—Alfred Wegener." Portsdown, *Moving Continents*. Last updated January 29, 2003. Available online. URL: http://www.bbm.me.uk/portsdown/PH_061_History_b.htm. Accessed December 8, 2007.

Brief description of Wegener's life, his theory, the ideas it attempted to replace, and contemporary scientists' reactions to it.

"Journey to the Center of the Earth." Physorg.com. February 21, 2008. Available online. URL: http://www.physorg.com/printnews. php?newsid=122821057. Accessed May 4, 2008.

A team of British and Swiss scientists have found new information about the way that pieces of Earth's crust sink into the mantle.

Kious, W. Jacqueline, and Robert I. Tilling. *This Dynamic Earth: The Story of Plate Tectonics*. U.S. Geological Survey. 1996, last updated January 29, 2001. Available online. URL: http://pubs.usgs.gov/gip/ dynamic. Accessed June 3, 2008.

Describes and illustrates the theory of plate tectonics, including the history of the theory's development from Alfred Wegener's theory of continental drift, and the effects of plate movement on human society.

"Meteorology—A Brief History." Florida State University Meteorology Department. Available online. URL: http://www.met.fsu.edu/explores/ methist.html. Accessed June 3, 2008.

A brief history of meteorology, the science of the atmosphere and weather, in which Alfred Wegener was a pioneer.

"Plate Tectonics." Crystalinks. Available online. URL: http://www. crystalinks.com/platetectonics.html. Accessed May 4, 2008.

Brief, illustrated description of the plate tectonics theory, including plate boundaries and the ways plates interact. The site also includes numerous links to current news stories about plate tectonics.

Sandwell, David T., and Walter H. F. Smith. "Exploring the Ocean Basins with Satellite Altimeter Data." National Geophysical Data Center, NOAA Satellite and Information Service. Last modified April 21, 2008. Available online. URL: http://www.ngdc.noaa.gov/mgg/bathymetry/ predicted/explore.html. Accessed May 4, 2008.

Describes information related to plate tectonics that has been obtained through satellites.

"The Story of Plate Tectonics." Available online. URL: http://www.plate tectonics.com. Accessed June 3, 2008.

Site includes a description of plate tectonics as well as an archive of articles and a book on the subject.

Periodicals

"Earth's Moving Crust May Occasionally Stop." *Space Daily,* January 10, 2008, n.p.

Two researchers conclude that plate movement may have occurred at different rates during different parts of the geologic past, sometimes even stopping entirely.

Ewing, Maurice, and Bruce C. Heezen. "Mid-Atlantic Ridge Seismic Belt." *Transactions of the American Geophysical Union* 37 (1956), 343 ff.

Scientific paper showing that the epicenters of earthquakes in the Atlantic Ocean lie along the center of the Mid-Atlantic Ridge.

"Finding Evidence of First Plate Tectonics." *Space Daily,* March 26, 2007, n. p.

Identification of the oldest preserved pieces of Earth's crust in southern Greenland offers evidence that the continents were moving 3.8 billion years ago, very early in the planet's history.

Hamilton, Warren. "Plate Tectonics—Its Influence on Man." *California Geology* 31 (October 1978): n.p. Also available online. URL: http://www.johnmartin.com/earthquakes/eqpapers/00000037.htm. Accessed June 8, 2008.

Describes concepts and development of the plate tectonics theory and the effects of plate movement on human society, for instance through deposition of valuable minerals and fossil fuels and, more negatively, through earthquakes and volcanic eruptions.

Hughes, Patrick. "The Meteorologist Who Started a Revolution." *Weatherwise* 51 (January–February 1998): 38–41.

Recounts Wegener's theory and explains why geologists and geophysicists of his time rejected it.

"In the Land of Death, Scientists Witness the Birth of a New Ocean." *Guardian,* November 2, 2006, n.p. Available online. URL: http://www.crystalinks.com/platetectonics.html. Accessed May 4, 2008.

The European Space Agency's Envisat satellite has spotted a huge rift opening beneath the Afar region of war-torn Ethiopia. The Nubian and Arabian tectonic plates are separating at this spot to create what will eventually be a new ocean.

Isacks, Bryan, Jack Oliver, and Lynn Sykes. "Seismology and the New Global Tectonics." *Journal of Geophysical Research* 73 (September 1967): 5,855–5,899.

> *First complete scientific summary of the theory of plate tectonics.*

Lawrence, David M. "Mountains under the Sea." *Mercator's World* 4 (November 1999): 36 ff.

> *Focuses on Marie Tharp's ocean maps and her discovery of the rift valley within the Mid-Atlantic Ridge.*

Pitman, W. C., III, and J. R. Heirtzler. "Magnetic Anomalies over the Pacific-Antarctic Ridge." *Science* 154 (December 2, 1966): 1,164–1,171.

> *Describes the* Eltanin *19 magnetic profile, whose perfect symmetry on the two sides of the ridge provided outstanding support for the seafloor spreading theory.*

Raff, A. D., and R. G. Mason. "Magnetic Survey off the West Coast of North America 32° N. Latitude to 42° N. Latitude." *Geological Society of America Bulletin* 72 (1961): 1,267–1,270.

> *First paper describing a striped pattern of magnetism in rocks around a mid-ocean ridge; such striping was later shown to reflect reversals in the Earth's magnetic field combined with creation of new crust through seafloor spreading.*

Vine, F. J. "Spreading of the Ocean Floor: New Evidence." *Science* 154 (December 16, 1966): 1,405–1,415.

> *Vine cites three independent confirmations of the Vine-Matthews-Morley theory: the magnetic profile he and John Tuzo Wilson took at the Juan de Fuca Ridge, the* Eltanin *19 profile, and the magnetic profiles from Neil Opdyke's sediment cores.*

———, and D. H. Matthews. "Magnetic Anomalies over Oceanic Ridges." *Nature* 199 (September 1963): 947–949.

> *Scientific paper showing how the existence of stripes of rocks with different magnetic alignments on the seafloor supports the theory of seafloor spreading.*

———, and John Tuzo Wilson. "Magnetic Anomalies over a Young Oceanic Ridge off Vancouver Island." *Science* 150 (October 22, 1965): 485–489.

> *In this paper, Vine and Wilson report a striped pattern of magnetism in seafloor rocks that supports the Vine-Matthews theory.*

Wilson, John Tuzo. "A New Class of Faults and Their Bearing on Continental Drift." *Nature* 207 (July 4, 1965): 343–347.

> *Wilson pictures the Earth's crust as being divided into rigid plates. He describes the plates' interaction and names a new kind of earthquake fault, the transform fault, which is formed when plates slide past one another.*

INDEX